ECONOMIC ISSUES, PROBLEMS AND PERSPECTIVES



# DEBT LIMIT MANAGEMENT AND THE GOVERNMENT'S ROLE

# ECONOMIC ISSUES, PROBLEMS AND PERSPECTIVES

Additional books in this series can be found on Nova's website under the Series tab.

Additional E-books in this series can be found on Nova's website under the E-books tab.

# AMERICAN POLITICAL, ECONOMIC, AND SECURITY ISSUES

Additional books in this series can be found on Nova's website under the Series tab.

Additional E-books in this series can be found on Nova's website under the E-books tab.

ECONOMIC ISSUES, PROBLEMS AND PERSPECTIVES

# DEBT LIMIT MANAGEMENT AND THE GOVERNMENT'S ROLE

JONATHAN D. ANTONELLIS
AND
NICHOLAS P. BARONE
EDITORS

Nova Science Publishers, Inc.
*New York*

**Library of Congress Cataloging-in-Publication Data**

Debt limit management and the government's role / editors, Jonathan D. Antonellis and Nicholas P. Barone.
p. cm.
Includes index.
ISBN 978-1-61324-418-0 (hardcover)
1. Debts, Public--United States--Management. 2. Budget--United States. 3. United States. Dept. of the Treasury. Office of Debt Management. I. Antonellis, Jonathan D. II. Barone, Nicholas P.
HJ8119.D423 2011
336.3'4350973--dc22

2011012603

*Published by Nova Science Publishers, Inc. ✝ New York*

# CONTENTS

# PREFACE

This book examines the possibility of the federal government reaching its statutory debt limit and not raising it, with a particular focus on government operations. The nature of the federal government's debt is explained, as are the processes associated with federal borrowing, and historical events that may influence prospective actions. This book also includes an analysis of what could happen if the federal government may no longer issue debt, has exhausted alternative sources of cash, and, therefore, depends on incoming receipts or other sources of funds to provide any cash needed to liquidate federal obligations.

Chapter 1 - The gross federal debt, which represents the federal government's total outstanding debt, consists of two types of debt: (1) debt held by the public and (2) debt held in government accounts, also known as intragovernmental debt. Federal government borrowing increases for two primary reasons: (1) budget deficits and (2) investments of any federal government account surpluses in Treasury securities, as required by law. Nearly all of this debt is subject to the statutory limit. The federal debt limit currently stands at $14,294 billion. Following current policy, Treasury has estimated that the debt limit will be reached in spring 2011.

Treasury has yet to face a situation in which it was unable to pay its obligations as a result of reaching the debt limit. In the past, the debt limit has always been raised before the debt reached the limit. However, on several occasions Treasury took extraordinary actions to avoid reaching the limit and, as a result, affected the operations of certain programs. If the Secretary of the Treasury determines that the issuance of obligations of the United States may not be made without exceeding the public debt limit, a debt issuance suspension period can be authorized. This gives Treasury the authority to utilize nontraditional methods to finance obligations.

Chapter 2 - Total debt of the federal government can increase in two ways. First, debt increases when the government sells debt to the public to finance budget deficits and acquire the financial resources needed to meet its obligations. This increases *debt held by the public*. Second, debt increases when the federal government issues debt to certain government accounts, such as the Social Security, Medicare, and Transportation trust funds, in exchange for their reported surpluses. This increases *debt held by government accounts*. The sum of *debt held by the public* and *debt held by government accounts* is the total federal debt. Surpluses reduce debt held by the public, while deficits raise it. Total federal debt outstanding was $14,104 billion on February 7, 2011. The U.S. Treasury projects the federal debt will reach its statutory limit in April or May 2011, although tax policy, spending changes, and economic trends, could affect that timing. Without a debt limit increase, funding federal operations after the middle of 2011 may be complicated.

Chapter 3 - GAO has prepared this report to assist Congress in identifying and addressing debt management challenges. Since 1995, the statutory debt limit has been increased 12 times to its current level of $14.294 trillion. The Department of the Treasury (Treasury) recently notified Congress that the current debt limit could be reached as early as April 5, 2011, and the Congressional Budget Office (CBO) projects that under current law debt subject to the limit will exceed $25 trillion in 2021.

Chapter 4 - The 2008 financial market crisis and the economic recession led to a rapid and substantial increase in federal debt. This report, part of a line of work on debt management, was conducted under the Comptroller General's authority. It describes current debt management challenges and examines the role of a program that could benefit Treasury—Treasury Inflation Protected Securities (TIPS). GAO analyzed market data and interviewed experts as well as the two largest holders of Treasury securities in each of six sectors.

In: Debt Limit Management...
Editors: J. D. Antonellis, N. P. Barone ISBN: 978-1-61324-418-0


*Chapter 1*

# REACHING THE DEBT LIMIT: BACKGROUND AND POTENTIAL EFFECTS ON GOVERNMENT OPERATIONS*

***Mindy R. Levit, Clinton T. Brass, Thomas J. Nicola, Dawn Nuschler and Alison M. Shelton***

## SUMMARY

The gross federal debt, which represents the federal government's total outstanding debt, consists of two types of debt: (1) debt held by the public and (2) debt held in government accounts, also known as intragovernmental debt. Federal government borrowing increases for two primary reasons: (1) budget deficits and (2) investments of any federal government account surpluses in Treasury securities, as required by law. Nearly all of this debt is subject to the statutory limit. The federal debt limit currently stands at $14,294 billion. Following current policy, Treasury has estimated that the debt limit will be reached in spring 2011.

Treasury has yet to face a situation in which it was unable to pay its obligations as a result of reaching the debt limit. In the past, the debt limit has always been raised before the debt reached the limit. However, on several occasions Treasury took extraordinary actions to avoid reaching the limit and, as a result, affected the operations of certain programs. If the Secretary of the Treasury determines that the issuance of obligations

---

* This is an edited, reformatted and augmented version of a Congressional Research Services publication, dated February 11, 2011.

of the United States may not be made without exceeding the public debt limit, a debt issuance suspension period can be authorized. This gives Treasury the authority to utilize nontraditional methods to finance obligations.

Treasury Secretary Geithner issued a letter to Congress on January 6, 2011, stating that Treasury has an ability to delay for several weeks the date by which the debt limit would be reached by taking certain actions. However, if these financing options are also exhausted and Treasury is no longer able to pay the bills, serious financial and economic implications could result that could have a lasting impact on federal programs and the U.S.'s ability to borrow in the future. According to Treasury, if the debt limit is not raised after that point, payment of other obligations and benefits would be discontinued, limited, or adversely affected. The letter also provided Treasury's views on the consequences of a default by the United States on its debt obligations.

Under current estimates, the federal government will have to issue an additional $738 billion in debt above the current statutory limit to finance obligations for the remainder of FY2011. If the debt limit is reached and Treasury is no longer able to issue federal debt, federal spending would have to be decreased or federal revenues would have to be increased by a corresponding amount to cover the gap in what cannot be borrowed. To put this into context, the federal government would have to eliminate all spending on discretionary programs, cut nearly 70% of outlays for mandatory programs, increase revenue collection by nearly two-thirds, or take some combination of those actions in the second half of FY2011(April through September 30, 2011) in order to avoid increasing the debt limit. Additional spending cuts and/or revenue increases would be required, under current policy, in FY2012 and beyond to avoid increasing the debt limit.

It is extremely difficult for Congress to effectively influence short-term fiscal and budgetary policy through action on legislation adjusting the debt limit. The need to raise (or lower) the limit during a session of Congress is driven by previous decisions regarding revenues and spending stemming from legislation enacted earlier in the session or in prior years. Nevertheless, the consideration of debt-limit legislation often is viewed as an opportunity to reexamine fiscal and budgetary policy. Consequently, House and Senate action on legislation adjusting the debt limit often is complicated, hindered by policy disagreements, and subject to delay. Which spending and revenue policies are enacted and how often Congress wishes to reconsider statutory debt limit legislation typically affects the level at which the debt limit is set.

# INTRODUCTION

The federal government's statutory debt limit is currently $14,294 billion (P.L. 111-139).[1] On January 6, 2011, Secretary of the Treasury Timothy Geithner issued a letter to Congress stating that the debt limit would be reached sometime between March 31 and May 16, 2011. Treasury has subsequently revised these estimates saying they now expect to reach the debt limit sometime between April 5, 2011, and May 31, 2011, due to an upward revision to projected receipts and a downward revision in projected debt to be issued to government trust funds.[2]

If the debt nears the legal limit and the debt limit is not increased, the Department of the Treasury (Treasury) would likely take actions outside of its typical cash management practices to pay federal obligations. Similar actions have been taken previously. If these financing options are exhausted and Treasury is no longer able to pay for all federal obligations, some federal payments to creditors, vendors, contractors, state and local governments, beneficiaries, and other entities would be delayed or limited. This could result in significant economic and financial consequences that may have a lasting impact on federal programs and the federal government's ability to borrow in the future.

This report examines the possibility of the federal government reaching its statutory debt limit and not raising it, with a particular focus on government operations. First, the report explains the nature of the federal government's debt, the processes associated with federal borrowing, and historical events that may influence prospective actions. It also includes an analysis of what *could* happen if the federal government may no longer issue debt, has exhausted alternative sources of cash, and, therefore, depends on incoming receipts or other sources of funds to provide any cash needed to liquidate federal obligations.[3] Finally this report lays out considerations for increasing the debt limit under current policy and what impact fiscal policy could have on the debt limit going forward.

# FEDERAL GOVERNMENT DEBT AND THE DEBT LIMIT[4]

The gross federal debt, which represents the federal government's total outstanding debt, consists of two types of debt:

- the debt held by the public and
- the debt held in government accounts, also known as intragovernmental debt.

Federal government borrowing increases for two primary reasons: (1) budget deficits and (2) investments of any federal government account surpluses in Treasury securities as required by law.[5]

The debt held by the public represents the total net amount borrowed from the public to cover the federal government's accumulated budget deficits. Annual budget deficits increase the debt held by the public by requiring the federal government to borrow additional funds to fulfill its commitments.

The debt held in government accounts represents the federal debt issued to certain accounts, primarily trust funds, such as those associated with Social Security, Medicare, and Unemployment Compensation. Generally, government account surpluses, which include trust fund surpluses, by law must be invested in special non-marketable federal government securities and thus are held in the form of federal debt.[6] Treasury periodically pays interest on the special securities held in a government account. Interest payments are typically paid in the form of additional special securities issued by Treasury to the trust funds, which also increases the amount of intragovernmental debt and federal debt subject to limit.

When a trust fund invests in U.S. Treasury securities, it effectively lends money to the rest of the government. The loan either reduces what the federal government must borrow from the public, if the budget is in deficit, or reduces the amount of publicly held debt, if the budget is in surplus. At the same time, the loan increases intragovernmental debt. The revenues exchanged for these securities then go into the General Fund of the Treasury and are indistinguishable from other cash in the General Fund. This cash may be used for any government spending purpose.[7]

Congress created a statutory debt limit in the Second Liberty Bond Act of 1917.[8] This development changed Treasury's borrowing process and assisted Congress in its efforts to exercise its constitutional prerogatives to control the federal government's fiscal outcomes. The debt limit also imposes a form of fiscal accountability that compels Congress and the President to take deliberate action to allow further federal borrowing if necessary.

Almost all of the federal government's borrowing is subject to a statutory limit.[9] From time to time, Congress has considered and adopted legislation to change this limit. Because the statutory limit applies to both debt held by the public and intragovernmental debt, both budget deficits and government account surpluses may contribute to the federal government reaching the existing debt limit.

## THE DEBT LIMIT AND THE TREASURY

Treasury's standard methods for financing federal activities can be disrupted when the level of federal debt nears its legal limit. If the limit prevents Treasury from issuing new debt to manage short-term cash flows or to finance an annual deficit, the government may be unable to obtain the cash needed to pay its bills. The limit may also prevent the government from issuing new debt in order to invest the surpluses of designated government accounts, such as federal trust funds. Treasury is caught between two requirements: the law that requires Treasury to pay the government's legal obligations or invest trust fund surpluses, on one hand, and the statutory debt limit which may prevent Treasury from issuing the debt to raise cash to pay obligations or make trust fund investments, on the other.[10]

The level of federal debt changes throughout the year due to fluctuations in income and outlays, whether or not the government has an annual surplus or deficit. Seasonal fluctuations could still require Treasury to sell debt even if the annual level of federal debt subject to limit does not increase (i.e., if the budget were balanced and trust funds were not in surplus). Even on a day-to-day basis, the level of federal debt can vary significantly. For example, Treasury issues large volumes of individual income tax refunds in February and March, because taxpayers expecting refunds tend to file early. On the other hand, Treasury tends to collect more revenue in April because taxpayers making payments tend to file closer to April 15.

Past Treasury Secretaries, when faced with a nearly binding debt ceiling, have used special strategies to handle cash and debt management responsibilities.[11] Since 1985, these measures have included

- suspending sales of nonmarketable debt (savings bonds, state and local government series, and other nonmarketable debt);
- trimming or delaying auctions of marketable securities;
- under-investing certain government funds (Social Security, Government Securities Investment Fund of the Federal Thrift Savings Plan, Exchange Stabilization Fund); and
- exchanging Treasury securities for non-Treasury securities held by the Federal Financing Bank (FFB).

Under current law, if the Secretary of the Treasury determines that the issuance of obligations of the United States may not be made without exceeding the debt limit, a "debt issuance suspension period" may be announced.[12] This gives Treasury the authority to suspend investments in, and prematurely redeem securities held by, the Civil Service Retirement and Disability Trust Fund. Debt issuance suspension periods were previously in effect from November 15, 1995, through January 15, 1997; April 4 through April 16, 2002; May 16 through June 28, 2002; and February 20 through May 27, 2003.

## Past Treasury Actions to Postpone Reaching the Debt Limit

Treasury has yet to face a situation in which it was unable to pay its obligations as a result of reaching the debt limit. However, during debt limit impasses in 1985, 1995-1996, 2002, and 2003, Treasury took extraordinary actions to avoid reaching the debt limit and to meet the federal government's other obligations. Some of the actions Treasury took during these periods are briefly discussed below, along with additional actions taken from 2009 to present.[13]

In September 1985, the Treasury Department informed Congress that it had reached the statutory debt limit. As a result, Treasury had to take extraordinary measures to meet the government's cash requirements. Treasury used various internal transactions involving the Federal Financing Bank (FFB) and delayed public auctions of government debt. It also was unable to issue, or had to delay issuing, new short-term government securities to the Civil Service Retirement and Disability Trust Fund, the Social Security Trust Funds, and several smaller trust funds. In particular, new Treasury obligations could not be issued to the trust funds because doing so would have exceeded the debt limit. Treasury took the additional step of "disinvesting" the Civil Service Retirement and Disability Trust Fund, the Social Security Trust Funds, and several smaller trust funds by redeeming some trust fund securities earlier than usual. Premature redemption of these securities created room under the debt ceiling for Treasury to borrow sufficient cash from the public to pay other obligations, including November Social Security benefits.[14] The debt limit was subsequently temporarily increased on November 14, 1985 (P.L. 99-155) and permanently increased on December 12, 1985 (P.L. 99-177) from $1,824 billion to $2,079 billion.

As a result of the 1985 debt limit crisis, Congress subsequently authorized the Treasury to alter its normal investment and redemption procedures for certain trust funds during a debt limit crisis. Such authority was not provided with respect to the Social Security trust funds. In addition, both P.L. 99-155 and P.L. 99-177 included provisions to require the Treasury to restore any interest income lost to the trust funds as a result of delayed investments and early redemptions.

During the debt limit crisis of 1995-1996, Treasury, once again, used nontraditional methods of financing, including some of the methods used during the 1985 crisis as well as not reinvesting some of the maturing Treasury securities held by the Exchange Stabilization Fund.[15] In early 1996, Treasury announced that it had insufficient cash to pay Social Security benefits for March 1996 because it was unable to issue new public debt.[16] To allow benefits to be paid in March 1996, Congress authorized the Treasury to issue securities to the public in the amount needed to make the March 1996 benefit payments and specified that, on a temporary basis, those securities would not count against the debt limit (P.L. 104-103 and P.L. 104-115). In 1996, Congress passed P.L. 104-121 to increase the debt limit and, among other provisions, to codify Congress's understanding that the Secretary of the Treasury and other federal officials are not authorized to use Social Security and Medicare funds for debt management purposes, except when necessary to provide for the payment of benefits or administrative expenses of the programs.

In addition, during periods in 2002 and 2003 (from April 4 through April 16, 2002; from May 16 through June 28, 2002; and from February 20 through May 27, 2003), Treasury again took actions to avoid reaching the debt limit, including utilizing certain trust fund assets and suspending the sale of securities to certain trust funds. The debt limit was permanently increased on June 28, 2002 (P.L. 107-199) from $5,950 billion to $6,400 billion and on May 27, 2003 (P.L. 108-24) from $6,400 billion to $7,384 billion.

Treasury used another tool in 2009 to cope with the debt limit without declaring a debt issuance suspension period. Specifically, Treasury used a program that was originally established as an alternative method for the Federal Reserve (Fed) to increase its assistance to the financial sector during the financial downturn, the Supplementary Financing Program (SFP), which was announced on September 17, 2008. Under the SFP, Treasury temporarily auctioned more new securities than were needed to finance government operations and deposited the proceeds at the Fed. Since January 2009, the Treasury has generally held $200 billion at the Fed under this program. When debt subject to limit approached the statutory debt limit around October 2009, however, Treasury withdrew all but $5 billion from the Fed to create room under the debt ceiling. Once the debt limit was raised on February 12, 2010, from $12,394 billion to $14,294 billion (P.L. 111-139), Treasury began increasing the balances held at the Fed back to $200 billion by issuing new debt to the public.

As discussed above, short delays in increasing the debt limit have caused the Treasury Secretary to take extraordinary actions to avoid disrupting the payments of federal obligations. Though the federal government incurred additional costs during these periods, such as disruption of government borrowing and trust fund investment programs, the payment of benefits and other outlays occurred largely on schedule and trust funds were made whole once these crises ended. However, if the budget continues to be in deficit and policy makers wish to avoid a default on federal obligations, such methods cannot avoid the eventual necessity of raising the debt limit.

### Current Treasury Actions in 2011 Surrounding the Debt Limit

Treasury Secretary Geithner's letter to Congress of January 6, 2011, states that Treasury has an ability to delay the date by which the current debt limit would be reached by utilizing similar methods used during past crises, including declaring a debt issuance suspension period, if necessary. According to Treasury, these actions could delay the date that the debt limit would be reached by several weeks. However, if the debt limit is not raised after that point, payment of other obligations and benefits would be "discontinued, limited, or adversely affected."[17]

## POTENTIAL IMPLICATIONS OF REACHING AND NOT RAISING THE DEBT LIMIT

If the federal government were to reach the debt limit and Treasury were to exhaust its alternative strategies for remaining under the debt limit, then the federal government would need to rely solely on incoming revenues to finance obligations. If this occurred during a period when the federal government was running a deficit, the dollar amount of newly incurred federal obligations would continually exceed the dollar amount of newly incoming revenues.

It is not possible for CRS to specifically predict what Congress, the President, the Office of Management and Budget (OMB), Treasury, federal agencies, and financial markets would do in certain situations. Nevertheless, it is possible to scope out some aspects of what *could* happen under a specific scenario, in which the federal government no longer may issue debt, has exhausted alternative sources of cash, and therefore is dependent upon incoming receipts or other sources of funds to provide any cash that is necessary to pay federal obligations. That said, CRS cannot state the full range of events that may occur if the described scenario were to actually take place.

## Possible Options for Treasury and OMB

In this scenario, the federal government implicitly would be required to use some sort of decision-making rule about whether to pay obligations in the order they are received, or, alternatively, to prioritize which obligations to pay, while other obligations would go into an unpaid queue. In other words, the federal government's inability to borrow or use other means of financing implies that payment of some or all bills or obligations would be delayed.

Treasury officials have maintained that the Department lacks formal legal authority to establish priorities to pay obligations, asserting, in effect, that each law obligating funds and authorizing expenditures stands on an equal footing.[18] In other words, Treasury would have to make payments on obligations as they came due. With regard to this view, Treasury recently noted that an attempt to prioritize payments was "unworkable" because adopting a policy that would require certain types of payments taking precedence over other U.S. legal obligations would merely be "a failure by the U.S. to stand behind its commitments."[19]

In contrast to this view, GAO wrote to then-Chairman Bob Packwood of the Senate Finance Committee in 1985 that it was aware of no requirement that Treasury must pay outstanding obligations in the order in which they are received.[20] GAO concluded that "Treasury is free to liquidate obligations in any order it finds will best serve the interests of the United States." In any case, if Treasury were to prioritize, it is not clear what the priorities might be among the different types of spending.[21]

It also is possible that OMB may use statutory authority to apportion or reapportion budget authority (i.e., the authority to incur obligations) that Congress has granted in appropriations, contract, and borrowing authority to delay expenditures and effectively establish priorities for liquidating obligations. OMB is required by statute to "apportion" these funds (e.g., quarterly) to prevent agencies from spending at a rate that would exhaust their appropriations before the end of the fiscal year.[22] If OMB were to use statutory apportionment authority to affect the rate of federal spending, its ability to do so would be constrained by the Impoundment Control Act of 1974, title X of the Congressional Budget and Impoundment Control Act of 1974 (P.L. 93-344).[23] The Impoundment Control Act does not prohibit the President from withholding funds, but establishes procedures for the President to submit formal requests to Congress either to defer (i.e., delay) spending until later or rescind (i.e., cancel) the budget authority that Congress previously had granted.[24] Although the use of OMB's apportionment authority in the event of a debt limit crisis might delay the need to pay some obligations, use of the authority would not prevent obligations from remaining unpaid.

## Potential Impacts on Government Operations

If the debt limit is reached and not increased, federal spending would be affected. Under normal circumstances, Treasury has sufficient financial resources to liquidate all obligations arising from discretionary and mandatory (direct) spending, the latter of which includes interest payments on the debt.[25] If a lapse in raising the debt limit should prevent Treasury from being able to liquidate all obligations on time, it is not clear whether the distinction between different types of spending would be significant or whether the need to establish priorities would disproportionately impact one type of spending or another. It is also not clear whether the distinctions among different types of obligations, such as contract, grant, benefit, and interest payments, would prove to be significant.

### *Potential Impacts on Programs Generally*

A government that delays paying its obligations in effect borrows from vendors, contractors, beneficiaries, other governments,[26] or employees who are not paid on time. Moreover, a backlog of unpaid bills would continue to grow until the government collects more revenues or other sources of cash than its outlays. In some cases, delaying federal payments incurs interest penalties under some statutes such as the Prompt Payment Act, which directs the government to pay interest penalties to contractors if it does not pay them by the required payment date,[27] and the Internal Revenue Code, which requires the government to pay interest penalties if tax refunds are delayed beyond a certain date.[28] The specific impacts of delayed payment would depend upon the nature of the federal program or activity for which funds are to be paid.

### *Potential Impacts on Programs with Trust Funds*

If Treasury delays investing a federal trust fund's revenues in government securities, or redeems prematurely a federal trust fund's holdings of government securities, the result would be a loss of interest to the affected trust fund. This could potentially worsen the financial situation of the affected trust fund(s) and accelerate insolvency dates.[29] As noted earlier, Congress passed P.L. 104-121 to prevent federal officials from using the Social Security and Medicare Trust Funds for debt management purposes, except when necessary to provide for the payment of benefits and administrative expenses of the programs. Under P.L. 99-509, Treasury is permitted to delay investment in the TSP's G-Fund and the Civil Service Retirement and Disability Trust Fund, and also to redeem prematurely assets of the Civil Service Retirement and Disability Trust Fund. However, the law also requires Treasury to make these funds whole after a debt limit impasse is resolved. The government maintains a number of other trust funds whose finances could potentially be harmed by delayed investment or early redemption in the absence of similar actions to make the trust funds whole after a debt limit impasse has ended.

### *Distinction Between a Debt Limit Crisis and a Government Shutdown*

In 1995, the Congressional Budget Office (CBO) contrasted this sort of scenario, under which the debt limit is reached and not raised, with a substantially different situation, in which the government must shut down due to lack of appropriations.

> Failing to raise the debt ceiling would not bring the government to a screeching halt the way that not passing appropriations bills would. Employees would not be sent home, and checks would continue to be issued. If the Treasury was low on cash, however, there could be delays in honoring checks and disruptions in the normal flow of government services.[30]

Alternatively stated, in a situation when the debt limit is reached and Treasury exhausts its financing alternatives, aside from ongoing cash flow, an agency may continue to obligate funds. However, Treasury may not be able to liquidate all obligations that result in federal outlays due to a shortage of cash. In contrast to this, if Congress and the President do not enact interim or full-year appropriations for an agency, the agency does not have budget authority available for obligation. If this occurs, the agency must shut down non-excepted activities, with immediate effects on government services.[31]

## Potential Economic and Financial Effects

In addition to the potential impact on federal programs and activities if the debt limit is not increased, there may also be economic and financial consequences. A 1979 GAO report described the consequences of failing to increase the debt ceiling. GAO said the government had never defaulted on any of its securities, because cash has been available to pay interest and redeem them upon maturity or demand.[32] Further, GAO said a default on the securities could have adverse effects on the economy, the public welfare, and the government's ability to market future securities.

> It is difficult to perceive all the adverse effects that a government default for even a short time would have on the economy and the public welfare. It is generally recognized that a default would preclude the government from honoring all of its obligations to pay for such things as employees' salaries and wages; social security benefits, civil service retirement, and other benefits from trust funds; contractual services and supplies, and maturing securities.... At a minimum, however, the government could be subject to additional claims for interest on unredeemed matured debt and to claims for damages resulting from failure to make payments. But even beyond that, the full faith and credit of the U.S. government would be threatened. Domestic money markets, in which government securities play a major role, could be affected substantially.[33]

If the debt limit were reached and interest payments on debt were paid, it is not clear what the repercussions would be on the financial markets or the economy. If Treasury had to rely on incoming cash to pay its obligations, a significant portion of government spending would go unpaid. Removing a portion of government spending from the economy would leave behind significant economic effects and would have an effect on GDP by definition, all other things being equal.[34] Further, if the government fails to make timely payments to individuals, service providers, and other organizations, these persons and entities would also be affected. Even if the government continued paying interest, it is not clear whether creditors would retain or lose faith in the government's willingness to pay its obligations. If creditors lost this confidence, the federal government's interest costs would likely increase substantially.

## CONSIDERATIONS FOR THE CURRENT DEBT LIMIT DEBATE

There are various viewpoints about how to deal with the current debt limit issues. The debt subject to limit will generally continue to rise as long as the budget remains in deficit or trust funds remain in surplus. To avoid raising the debt limit and continue normal government operations, significant spending cuts and/or revenue increases would be required.

### Illustrations of Contrasting Perspectives[35]

Various members of the Obama Administration have stated that the consequences of a federal default would be serious. Treasury Secretary Geithner's letter of January 6, 2011, provided Treasury's views on the "consequences of default by the United States," describing, among other things, payments that would be "discontinued, limited, or adversely affected."[36] The letter also said a short-term or limited default on legal obligations would cause "catastrophic damage to the economy."[37] Chairman of the White House Council of Economic Advisers Austan Goolsbee elaborated, saying that a default would cause "a worse financial economic crisis than anything we saw in 2008."[38] Secretary Geithner, in his letter to Congress added, "Default would have prolonged and far-reaching negative consequences on the safe-haven status of Treasuries and the dollar's dominant role in the international financial system, causing further increases in interest rates and reducing the willingness of investors here and around the world to invest in the United States...."[39] In a later online posting, Treasury Deputy Secretary Neal Wolin wrote that proposals to prioritize payments on the national debt above other legal obligations would not prevent default and would bring the same economic consequences Secretary Geithner described.[40] Looking forward, Secretary Geithner said in his letter that in addition to addressing the debt limit, the President wants to work with Congress to address the federal government's fiscal position with particular attention to addressing "medium- and long-term fiscal challenges."[41]

Other policy makers have expressed some contrasting perspectives focusing on the need to tie proposals to raise the debt limit to spending cuts, changes to the budget process, or instructions on how to deal with the payment of obligations if the debt limit is reached. For example, Senator Jim DeMint wrote in an op-ed that a vote to raise the debt limit should be opposed "unless Congress first passes a balanced-budget amendment that requires a two-thirds majority to raise taxes."[42] Other proposals also have emerged. Senator Pat Toomey and Representative Tom McClintock introduced legislation that, in the event of a debt limit crisis, would require Treasury to make payment of principal and interest on debt held by the public a higher priority than all other federal government obligations (S. 163/H.R. 421; 112th Congress). In a letter to Secretary Geithner, Senator Toomey said "This legislation is designed to maintain orderly financial markets by reassuring investors in U.S. Treasury securities that their investments are perfectly safe even in the unlikely event that the debt limit is temporarily reached."[43] Similarly, Senator David Vitter introduced legislation that would require priority be given to payment of all obligations on the debt held by the public and Social Security benefits in the event that the debt limit is reached (S. 259; 112th Congress).

Economists have expressed concern regarding the current level of federal debt. However, they maintain that there would be significant consequences if the debt limit is not raised. Federal Reserve Chairman Ben Bernanke has stated that Congress must work to put a plan in to place that would lower the nation's federal debt. He also stated that not raising the debt limit could ultimately lead the nation to default on its debt with catastrophic implications for the financial system and the economy.[44] Mark Zandi, chief economist for Moody's Analytics, expressed similar sentiments regarding the debt limit and the potential impact on the economy. He stated, "Global investors are already anxious regarding our ability to come to a political consensus to address the nation's fiscal challenges; a protracted debate over the debt ceiling would be very counterproductive."[45] Donald Marron, the director of the Urban-Brookings Tax Policy Center and a former acting director of the Congressional Budget Office, recently expressed similar views. He stated, "Geithner is correct that the debt limit must increase. With monthly deficits running more than $100 billion, it's simply unthinkable that Congress could cut spending or increase revenue enough to avoid borrowing more.... Still, I am troubled by any suggestion that the United States might willingly default on its public debt. Doing so would have absolutely no upside."[46]

## Can an Increase in the Current Debt Limit be Avoided?

Under current estimates, the federal government will have to issue an additional $738 billion in debt on net above the current statutory limit to finance all obligations for the remainder of FY2011.[47] If the debt limit is reached and Treasury is no longer able to issue federal debt, federal spending would have to be decreased or federal revenues would have to be increased by a corresponding amount to cover the gap in what cannot be borrowed. To put this into context, the federal government is expected to spend roughly $688 billion on discretionary programs and $1,054 billion on mandatory programs in the second half of FY2011. If the debt limit were not raised and all discretionary spending in the second half of the fiscal year were eliminated, the federal government would still have to find further savings to cover its borrowing needs. Alternatively, the federal government would be able to cover its borrowing needs by cutting nearly 70% of outlays for mandatory programs in the second half of FY2011 (April through September 30, 2011).

In terms of revenues, the federal government is expected to collect roughly $1,114 billion in the second half of FY2011 (April through September 30, 2011). To cover the $738 billion in borrowing needs solely by increasing revenues, the government would have to raise taxes by about two-thirds. These spending cuts and revenue increases provide an approximation of what would be required to cover the borrowing need for the remainder of FY2011under current policy. They do not address what would be required in FY2012 and beyond to avoid having to raise the debt limit.

## How Much Should the Debt Limit Be Raised?

Under current policy, the debt subject to limit is projected to increase throughout the remainder of the decade. The debt subject to limit is projected to reach $15,032 billion at the end of FY2011.[48] Under President Obama's FY2011 budget proposals, it is projected to reach $26,200 billion at the end of FY2020.[49] This represents an increase of over $1 trillion in each fiscal year during the FY2011 to FY2020 period. Increases in debt subject to limit at this level occur even as the budget deficit is projected to decline, in nominal dollars, between FY2011 and FY2014. Between FY2015 and FY2018, the budget deficit is projected to remain roughly stable, before rising thereafter.[50] In other words, the debt subject to limit increases even if the budget deficit declines in nominal terms as issuing debt would still be required to finance federal spending in excess of federal revenues (i.e., budget deficits).

Given the borrowing requirements discussed above, the current estimates stipulate the increases in the debt limit that would be required. However, depending on the spending and revenue proposals that may be subsequently enacted, borrowing requirements could change going forward. These borrowing requirements will dictate the level of debt and subsequent future increases in the debt limit. How often Congress wishes to reconsider statutory debt limit legislation typically affects the level at which the debt limit is set.

Temporary increases in the debt limit have been used in the past to provide additional time for Congress to consider debt limit increases. However, past temporary debt limit increases were eventually followed by permanent increases. If a temporary increase were to expire and the debt limit were to revert to a prior lower level, Congress may want to enact legislation that would result in a budget surplus in excess of the intragovernmental surplus in order to lower the level of debt subject to limit. If this legislation is not enacted and fully realized prior to the expiration of the temporary limit, then the level of debt would exceed the lowered debt limit.

## IMPLICATIONS OF FUTURE FEDERAL DEBT ON THE DEBT LIMIT

It is extremely difficult for Congress to effectively influence short-term fiscal and budgetary policy through action on legislation adjusting the debt limit. For example, the debt is projected to reach the current limit after spending and revenue decisions for half of the current fiscal year have already been made. The need to raise (or lower) the limit during a session of Congress is driven by previous decisions regarding revenues and spending. These decisions stem from legislation enacted earlier in the session or in prior years. Nevertheless, the consideration of debt limit legislation often is viewed as an opportunity to reexamine fiscal and budgetary policy. Consequently, House and Senate action on legislation adjusting the debt limit often is complicated, hindered by policy disagreements, and subject to delay.[51]

Generally, the following scenarios dictate whether or not an increase in the debt limit would be necessary, all else constant:

- If the federal budget is in deficit and intragovernmental debt is rising, an increase in the debt limit would be necessary.
- If the federal budget is in deficit and intragovernmental debt falls by an amount that is smaller than the budget deficit, an increase in the debt limit would be necessary.
- If the federal budget is balanced or in surplus and intragovernmental debt rises by an amount that is larger than the budget surplus, an increase in the debt limit would be necessary.
- If the federal budget is balanced or in surplus and intragovernmental debt is falling, an increase in the debt limit would not be required.

In other words, increases in the statutory debt limit would be required if the budget remains in deficit, even if future deficit levels are lower than they are at present, or if there are increases in the level of intragovernmental debt. If intragovernmental debt is declining, presumably due to the need of certain trust funds to redeem their holdings of Treasury securities in order to pay benefits, the Treasury would have to provide the trust funds with cash either from the General Fund resources or by issuing additional debt to the public to raise cash. If the federal budget is in deficit, Treasury would have to raise the necessary cash to redeem trust fund securities by issuing debt to the public. This would not require an increase in the debt limit, as the decline in intragovernmental debt would be offset by an equal increase in debt held by the public. A decline in intragovernmental debt as a result of a redemption in trust fund securities could be financed by using surplus cash if the federal budget is in surplus at that time.[52] In this situation both debt held by the public and total federal debt would decrease. If the budget surplus were less than the reduction in intragovernmental debt, the increase in the debt held by the public would be offset by the decline in intragovernmental debt, resulting in a decrease in the total debt.

# Appendix. Detailed History on Past Treasury Actions During Previous Debt Limit Crises

## Selected Actions in 1985

In September 1985, the Treasury Department informed Congress that it had reached the statutory debt limit. As a result, Treasury had to take extraordinary measures to meet the government's cash requirements. Treasury used various internal transactions involving the Federal Financing Bank (FFB) and delayed public auctions of government debt. It also was unable to issue, or had to delay issuing, new short-term government securities to the Civil Service Retirement and Disability Trust Fund, the Social Security Trust Funds, and several smaller trust funds. Issuing new government securities to the trust funds would have caused the federal debt to exceed the debt limit. During this period, the bulk of Social Security payroll tax revenues were kept in a non-interest bearing account.

Treasury took the additional step of "disinvesting" the Civil Service Retirement and Disability Trust Fund, the Social Security Trust Funds, and several smaller trust funds by redeeming some trust fund securities earlier than usual. Premature redemption of these securities created room under the debt ceiling for Treasury to borrow sufficient cash from the public to pay other obligations, including November Social Security benefits.[53]

As a result of these various actions, Social Security benefit payments and other federal payments were not jeopardized. The debt limit was subsequently temporarily increased on November 14, 1985 (P.L. 99-155) and permanently increased on December 12, 1985 (P.L. 99-177) from $1,824 billion to $2,079 billion. Both P.L. 99-155 and P.L. 99-177 included provisions to require the Treasury to restore any interest income lost to the trust funds as a result of delayed investments and early redemptions.

Concerning the Treasury's management of the Social Security Trust Funds during the 1985 debt limit impasse, the General Accounting Office (GAO, now the Government Accountability Office) wrote: "We conclude that, although some of the Secretary's actions appear in retrospect to have been in violation of the requirements of the Social Security Act, we cannot say that the Secretary acted unreasonably given the extraordinary situation in which he was operating."[54] In particular, GAO found that not all the delayed investment and securities redemptions during the period from September through November 1985 were necessary to meet Social Security benefit payments, and the excess was used to finance general government operations.[55]

Following the 1985 debt limit crisis, Congress formally authorized the Secretary of the Treasury to declare a debt issuance suspension period and, during such periods, to depart from normal trust fund investment practices with respect to certain funds such as the Civil Service Retirement and Disability Fund and the TSP's G Fund (P.L. 99-509, the Omnibus Budget Reconciliation Act of 1986). Funds raised by procedures authorized during a debt issuance suspension period can only be used to the extent necessary to prevent the public debt from exceeding the debt limit. After the debt issuance suspension period has ended, P.L. 99-509 requires Treasury to make the trust funds whole by issuing the appropriate amount of securities and crediting any interest lost due to non-investment or early disinvestment of these funds.[56] Such authority to depart from normal trust fund investment practices was not provided with respect to the Social Security Trust Funds. A provision to allow such authority was dropped from P.L. 99-509 during conference.

## Selected Actions in 1995-1996

Following the enactment of this additional authority, the first debt issuance suspension period was announced on November 15, 1995. Treasury, once again, used non-traditional methods of financing, including some of the methods used during the 1985 crisis as well as not reinvesting some of the maturing Treasury securities held by the Exchange Stabilization Fund.[57] In addition, Treasury utilized the new authority that was enacted under P.L. 99-509 to declare a debt issuance suspension period.

In early 1996, Treasury announced that it had insufficient cash to pay Social Security benefits for March 1996.[58] Congress responded on February 1, 1996, by passing P.L. 104-103, which provided the Treasury with temporary authority to issue securities to the public in an amount equal to the March 1996 Social Security benefit payments. Treasury issued about $29 billion of securities on February 23, 1996, and, under P.L. 104-103, these new securities were not to count against the debt limit until March 15, 1996. On March 7, 1996, Congress passed P.L. 104-115, which amended P.L. 104-103 to permit Treasury to continue investing payroll tax revenues in government securities and also to extend the exemption of the securities issued under P.L. 104- 103 from counting against the debt limit until March 30, 1996.

The debt limit was permanently increased on March 29, 1996 (P.L. 104-121) from $4,900 billion to $5,500 billion. P.L. 104-121 also codified Congress's understanding that the Secretary of the Treasury and other Federal officials are not authorized to use Social Security and Medicare funds for debt management purposes.[59] SSA states the following:

> Specifically, the Secretary of the Treasury and other federal officials are required not to delay or otherwise underinvest incoming receipts to the Social Security and Medicare Trust Funds. They are also required not to sell, redeem, or otherwise disinvest securities, obligations, or other assets of these Trust Funds except when necessary to provide for the payment of benefits and administrative expenses of the programs.[60]

These restrictions apply to the Federal Old-Age and Survivors Insurance (OASI) Trust Fund, the Federal Disability Insurance (DI) Trust Fund, the Federal Hospital Insurance (HI) Trust Fund, and the Federal Supplementary Medical Insurance (SMI) Trust Fund.

## Social Security Trust Fund Cash and Investment Management Practices under Normal Procedures and when Approaching the Debt Limit

By law, the Social Security Trust Funds must be invested in interest-bearing obligations of the United States or in obligations guaranteed as to both principal and interest by the United States (42 U.S.C. § 401(d) and 42 U.S.C. § 1320b-15).[61] The securities that the Treasury issues to the Social Security Trust Funds count toward the federal debt limit.

Under normal procedures, Social Security revenues (Social Security payroll taxes and individual income taxes) are immediately credited to the Social Security Trust Funds in the form of short-term, non-marketable Treasury securities called certificates of indebtedness (CIs). Under the terms of this exchange, when Treasury credits payroll tax and other revenues to Social Security in the form of CIs, the revenues themselves become available in the General Fund for other government operations.

CIs generally mature on the following June 30. Each June 30, any surplus for the year is converted from short-term Treasury securities to long-term, non-marketable Treasury securities called "special-issue obligations" or "specials."[62] In addition, other special issues that have just matured and that are not needed to pay near-term benefits are reinvested in special-issue obligations. Interest income is credited to the trust funds semi-annually (on June 30 and December 31) in the form of additional special-issue obligations.[63]

Social Security benefits are paid by the Treasury from the General Fund. When Treasury pays Social Security benefits, it redeems an equivalent amount of Treasury securities held by the trust funds in order to reimburse the General Fund.

In 2011, when the federal government is expected to reach the current debt ceiling, the Social Security program is projected to run a cash deficit. That is, Social Security's tax revenues are projected to be less than outlays for benefit payments and administration.[64] In a year when Social Security runs a cash flow deficit, the Treasury redeems some long-term government securities held by the trust funds. However, Social Security will still need to invest in non-marketable, short-term government securities in 2011 to manage short-term cash flows during the periods between receiving revenues and paying benefits (42 U.S.C. § 401(a), 42 U.S.C. § 401(d) and 42 U.S.C. § 1320b-15). Investing the trust funds' revenues for even very short periods ensures that the trust funds maximize their interest earnings. Social Security will also need to invest in non-marketable, long-term government securities in June 2011 when short-term and certain long-term trust fund securities mature in June and amounts not needed to pay near-term benefits are rolled over into long-term government securities, and in June and December 2011 when semi-annual interest income is paid and interest income that is not needed to pay near-term benefits is invested in long-term government securities.

In addition, Social Security will draw on general revenues as a result of the Tax Relief, Unemployment Insurance Reauthorization, and Job Creation Act of 2010 (P.L. 111-312, signed on December 17, 2010). Among other provisions, P.L. 111-312 provides a temporary 2 percentage point reduction in the Social Security payroll tax for employees and the self-employed in 2011, resulting in a tax rate of 4.2% for employees and 10.4% for the self-employed.[65] To protect the Social Security Trust Funds from a loss of payroll tax revenues, P.L. 111-312 appropriates to the Social Security Trust Funds amounts equal to the reduction in payroll tax revenues. The law specifies that these appropriated amounts "shall be transferred from the General Fund at such times and in such manner as to replicate to the extent possible the transfers which would have occurred to such Trust Fund had such amendments not been enacted."[66]

Depending on the extent and duration of any future debt limit crisis, and also on Treasury prioritization decisions, Social Security trust fund investment management procedures and benefit payments potentially could be affected because of the requirement that Treasury obligations cannot be issued to the Social Security trust funds if doing so would exceed the debt limit.[67] Absent Congressional action to make the trust funds whole, delayed issuance of government obligations to the trust funds, or early redemption of some trust fund assets, could accelerate depletion of the trust funds and move up the expected insolvency date.

Depending on the government's cash position in a given month, Treasury may need to issue new public debt to raise the cash needed to pay benefits. Treasury may be unable to issue new public debt, however, if doing so would exceed the debt limit. Social Security benefit payments may be delayed or jeopardized if the Treasury does not have enough cash on hand to pay benefits.

## End Notes

[1] The statutory debt limit may be compared with the current level of "debt subject to limit" in U.S. Department of the Treasury, *Daily Treasury Statement*, Table III-C, available at http://fms.treas.gov/dts/index.html.

[2] Letter from Timothy F. Geithner, Secretary of the Treasury, to the Hon. Harry Reid, Senate majority leader, January 6, 2011, available at http://www.treasury.gov/connect/ blog/Pages/letter.aspx. U.S. Department of the Treasury, *Treasury Assistant Secretary for Financial Markets Mary Miller February 2011 Quarterly Refunding Statement*, February 2, 2011, available at http://www.treasury.gov/press-center/press-releases/Pages/tg1045.aspx.

[3] The possible scenario sometimes has been referred to generically as a debt limit crisis. U.S. General Accounting Office (now the Government Accountability Office and hereafter GAO), *Debt Ceiling: Analysis of Actions During the 2003 Debt Issuance Suspension Periods*, GAO-04-526, May 2004.

[4] This section draws on CRS Report 98-453, *Debt-Limit Legislation in the Congressional Budget Process*, by Bill Heniff Jr., and CRS Report RL31967, *The Debt Limit: History and Recent Increases*, by D. Andrew Austin and Mindy R. Levit.

[5] If the budget is in surplus and intragovernmental debt rises by an amount that is less than the budget surplus, the total debt would not increase. See the later discussion in the section titled "Implications of Future Federal Debt on the Debt Limit."

[6] GAO, *Federal Trust and Other Earmarked Funds Answers to Frequently Asked Questions*, GAO-01-199SP, January 2001, pp. 17-18.

[7] For an explanation of how this process works for the Social Security trust funds, see Appendix.

[8] Chapter 56, 40 Stat. 288 (1917). The debt limit is now codified at 31 U.S.C. § 3101.

[9] The Treasury defines "Total Public Debt Subject to Limit" as "the Total Public Debt Outstanding less Unamortized Discount on Treasury Bills and Zero-Coupon Treasury Bonds, old debt issued prior to 1917, and old currency called United States Notes, as well as Debt held by the Federal Financing Bank and Guaranteed Debt." Approximately 0.5% of total federal debt is not subject to the debt limit. For more information, see U.S. Office of Management and Budget (hereafter OMB), *Budget of the U.S. Government, Analytical Perspectives*, Chapter 6 and Table 6-2.

[10] *See generally,* 31 U.S.C. §§ 3321 *et seq.* for the Treasury Secretary's duty to pay obligations. Regarding trust fund investments, see, for example, 42 U.S.C. § 401 (Social Security Trust Funds) and 5 U.S.C. § 8348 (Civil Service Retirement and Disability Trust Fund). The debt limit is codified at 31 U.S.C. § 3101.

[11] For example, see archived CRS Report 95-1109, *Authority to Tap Trust Funds and Establish Payment Priorities if the Debt Limit is not Increased*, by Thomas J. Nicola and Morton Rosenberg (available from CRS upon request).

[12] Congress formally authorized the additional powers to the Treasury Secretary under a "debt issuance suspension period" in the Omnibus Budget Reconciliation Act of 1986 (P.L. 99-509).

[13] For a more detailed analysis of past Treasury actions surrounding the debt limit impasses of 1985 and 1995-1996, see the Appendix.

[14] Treasury also redeemed some of the Social Security Trust Funds' holdings of long-term securities to reimburse the General Fund for cash payments of benefits in September through November 1985. As described above, during this period, the Treasury was unable to follow its normal procedure of issuing short-term securities to the trust funds and then

redeeming short-term securities to reimburse the General Fund when it paid Social Security benefits.

[15] Treasury's Exchange Stabilization Fund buys and sells foreign currency to promote exchange rate stability and counter disorderly conditions in the foreign exchange market.

[16] As described in the Appendix, under normal procedures Treasury pays Social Security benefits from the General Fund and offsets this by redeeming an equivalent amount of the trust funds' holdings of government debt. In order to pay Social Security benefits, and depending on the government's cash position at the time, Treasury may need to issue new public debt to raise the cash needed to pay benefits. Treasury may be unable to issue new public debt, however, because of the debt limit. Social Security benefit payments may be delayed or jeopardized if the Treasury does not have enough cash on hand to pay benefits.

[17] Letter from Timothy F. Geithner, Secretary of the Treasury, to the Hon. Harry Reid, Senate majority leader, January 6, 2011, p. 4, available at http://www.treasury.gov/ connect/blog/ Pages/letter.aspx.

[18] U.S. Congress, Senate Committee on Finance, *Increase of Permanent Public Debt Limit*, S.Rpt. 99-144, September 26, 1985. For more information, see archived CRS Report 95-1109, *Authority to Tap Trust Funds and Establish Payment Priorities if the Debt Limit is Not Increased*, by Thomas J. Nicola and Morton Rosenberg (available from CRS upon request).

[19] "Treasury: Proposals to 'Prioritize' Payments on U.S. Debt Not Workable: Would Not Prevent Default," Neal Wolin, Deputy Secretary of the Treasury, January 21, 2011, at http://www.treasury.gov/connect/blog/Pages/Proposals-toPrioritize-Payments-on-US-Debt-Not-Workable-Would-Not-Prevent-Default.aspx.

[20] Letter from GAO to the Hon. Bob Packwood, chairman of Senate Finance Committee, GAO B-138524, October 9, 1985, at http://redbook.gao.gov/14/fl0065142.php.

[21] While CRS has not located a list of established priorities to pay bills during a lapse in increasing the debt limit, OMB previously prepared a list of essential functions that the government should continue to conduct during a government shutdown caused by a lapse in enacting appropriations. These priorities are based on a distinction between functions deemed excepted, such as providing health care or air traffic control, and those deemed non-excepted. If it should become necessary to establish priorities to pay bills when the debt limit has not been increased, it is possible that the Secretary of the Treasury may look to this list of essential functions for some guidance. See later discussion in the section titled "Distinction Between a Debt Limit Crisis and a Government Shutdown."

[22] 31 U.S.C. § 1512, a provision of the Antideficiency Act, for example, states that appropriations for a definite period must be apportioned by such things as months, activities, or a combination of them to avoid obligation at a rate that would indicate a necessity of a deficiency or supplemental appropriations for the period. While apportionment commonly is used to control the rate at which agencies are allowed to *obligate* funds such as by placing orders and signing contracts, the text of Section 1512 also provides that it may be used to avoid *expending* funds.

[23] 2 U.S.C. §§ 681-692. During the period leading up to enactment of the Impoundment Control Act of 1974, the Nixon Administration used apportionment authority as a tool ultimately to limit outlays to conform to the President's budgetary priorities. Several lawsuits were brought to challenge the President's authority not to expend funds that Congress had appropriated and some lower courts held that the President lacked this authority. The Supreme Court did not address the merits of this issue.

[24] Generally, funds that have been proposed for deferral or rescission must be withheld for 45 days of continuous legislative session (excluding periods of more than three days when Congress is not in session), after which period they must be released unless Congress enacts a joint resolution to acquiesce in whole or in part to these requests. Congress sometimes responds to presidential deferral or rescission requests by acting on bills to defer or rescind different budget authorities from the ones that the President has proposed. Because deferrals or rescissions proposed by the President do not take effect unless Congress acquiesces to them, Congress as a matter of law has the final say on these matters. In practice, however, funds that are subject to these presidential requests often are withheld for long periods. For more information, see CRS Report RL33869, *Rescission Actions Since 1974: Review and Assessment of the Record*, by Virginia A. McMurtry.

[25] Discretionary spending is provided in, and controlled by, annual appropriations acts, which fund many of the routine activities commonly associated with such federal government functions as running executive branch agencies, congressional offices and agencies, and international operations of the government. Mandatory spending includes federal government spending on entitlement programs as well as other budget outlays controlled by laws other than appropriations acts. Mandatory spending also includes appropriated entitlements, such as Medicaid and certain veterans' programs, which are funded in annual appropriations acts. For more information, see CRS Report RS20129, *Entitlements and Appropriated Entitlements in the Federal Budget Process*, by Bill Heniff Jr.

[26] For example, because federal, state, and local government finances are linked by various intergovernmental transfers, late payment or nonpayment of federal obligations to states could affect the budgets and finances of local governments, such as school districts, counties, and municipalities.

[27] 31 U.S.C. § 3902.

[28] 26 U.S.C. § 6611.

[29] For information about the balances of all federal trust funds, see CRS Report R41328, *Federal Trust Funds and the Budget*, by Thomas L. Hungerford. [30] Congressional Budget Office (hereafter, CBO), *The Economic and Budget Outlook: An Update*, August 1995, p. 49.

[31] In the event of a funding hiatus, the Antideficiency Act nevertheless allows an exception for agencies to incur obligations for emergencies involving the safety of human life or the protection of property. For discussion, see CRS Report RL34680, *Shutdown of the Federal Government: Causes, Processes, and Effects*, by Clinton T. Brass.

[32] While this passage indicates that a delay in increasing the debt limit has the potential to postpone the payment of Social Security benefits, among other benefits, Social Security benefits have been paid on time during past debt limit crises. Non-marketable securities can be redeemed on demand. GAO, *A New Approach to the Public Debt Legislation Should be Considered*, FGMSD-79-58, September 1979, pp. 17-18, http://archive.gao.gov/f0302/110373.pdf.

[39] Treasury Secretary Geithner letter, January 6, 2011, p. 4.

[40] Neal Wolin, Deputy Secretary of the Treasury, "Treasury: Proposals to 'Prioritize' Payments on U.S. Debt Not Workable; Would Not Prevent Default," January 21, 2011, at http://www.treasury.gov/connect/blog/Pages/Proposalsto-Prioritize-Payments-on-US-Debt-Not-Workable-Would-Not-Prevent-Default.aspx.

[41] Treasury Secretary Geithner letter, January 6, 2011, p. 4.

[42] Senator Jim DeMint, "More Spending is a Threat to America," *Politico*, January 24, 2011, at http://www.politico.com/news/stories/0111/48020.html.

[43] Senator Pat Toomey, "Senator Toomey Sends Letter to Secretary Geithner on the Debt Limit," press release, February 2, 2011, http://toomey.senate.gov/record.cfm?id=330828&.

[44] Davidson, Paul, "Economy still in a deep hole, Bernanke says," USA Today, February 4, 2011.

[45] U.S. Congress, Senate Committee on the Budget, *Challenges for the U.S. Economic Recovery*, Testimony of Mark Zandi, February 3, 2011, available at http://budget.senate.gov/democratic/testimony/2011/ Zandi_Senate_Budget_2_3_2011.pdf.

[46] Marron, Donald, "Debt Ceiling: Geithner Won't Let Us Default," *CNNMoney.com*, January 19, 2011.

[47] The amount of federal borrowing needed to fulfill obligations through the end of the fiscal year may depend on Treasury's use of the supplemental financing program. CRS calculations based on U.S. Congressional Budget Office, *The Budget and Economic Outlook: Fiscal Years 2011 to 2021*, January 2011, Tables 1-4 and C-2.

[48] U.S. Congressional Budget Office, *The Budget and Economic Outlook: Fiscal Years 2011 to 2021*, January 2011, Table C-2.

[49] Office of Management and Budget, *Budget of the U.S. Government, Fiscal Year 2011, Mid-Session Review*, Table S-14, available at http://www.whitehouse.gov/sites/ default/files/omb/budget/fy2011/assets/11msr.pdf.

[50] Office of Management and Budget, *Budget of the U.S. Government, Fiscal Year 2011, Mid-Session Review*, Table S-1.

[51] For more information, see CRS Report RS21519, *Legislative Procedures for Adjusting the Public Debt Limit: A Brief Overview*, by Bill Heniff Jr.

[33] Ibid.

[34] GDP = consumption + investment + government spending + (exports – imports). If government spending declines, then GDP will also decline by definition, all else equal.

[35] This report focuses on the potential impacts on government operations of reaching the debt limit and does not analyze or track proposals from the Administration or Congress in how to approach the debt limit issue.

[36] Letter from Timothy F. Geithner, Secretary of the Treasury, to the Hon. Harry Reid, Senate majority leader, January 6, 2011, p. 4.

[37] Ibid., pp. 1, 3.

[38] ABC News *This Week*, Transcript: White House Adviser Austan Goolsbee, January 2, 2011, at http://abcnews.go.com/ThisWeek/week-transcript-white-house-adviser-austan-goolsbee/story?id=12522822.

[52] Under the most recent projections, the federal budget is expected to remain in deficit through FY2021 under current law. U.S. Congressional Budget Office, *The Budget and Economic Outlook: Fiscal Years 2011 to 2021*, January 2011, Table 1-1.

[53] Treasury redeemed some of the Social Security Trust Funds' holdings of long-term securities to reimburse the General Fund for cash payments of benefits in September through November 1985. As described above, during this period, the Treasury was unable to follow its normal procedure of issuing short-term securities to the trust funds and then redeeming short-term securities to reimburse the General Fund when it paid Social Security benefits.

[54] Letter from Charles A. Bowsher, Comptroller General of the United States, to the Hon. James R. Jones, chairman, Subcommittee on Social Security, House Committee on Ways and Means, December 5, 1985, GAO B-221077.2, http://archive.gao.gov/d12t3/128621.pdf.

[55] Ibid.

[56] GAO, *Debt Ceiling Options*, AIMD-96-20R, December 7, 1995, http://archive.gao.gov/paprpdf1/155750.pdf.

[57] Treasury's Exchange Stabilization Fund buys and sells foreign currency to promote exchange rate stability and counter disorderly conditions in the foreign exchange market.

[58] As described in later in this Appendix, under normal procedures Treasury pays Social Security benefits from the General Fund and offsets this by redeeming an equivalent amount of the trust funds' holdings of government debt. In order to pay Social Security benefits, and depending on the government's cash position at the time, Treasury may need to issue new public debt to raise the cash needed to pay benefits. Treasury may be unable to issue new public debt, however, because of the debt limit. Social Security benefit payments may be delayed or jeopardized if the Treasury does not have enough cash on hand to pay benefits.

[59] See 42 U.S.C. § 1320b-15.

[60] U.S. Social Security Administration, "Program Legislation Enacted in Early 1996," *Social Security Bulletin*, vol. 59, no. 2, Summer 1996, p. 65, at http://www.ssa.gov/policy

[61] There are two sources of Social Security revenues: (1) payroll taxes paid by workers and employers and (2) federal income taxes paid by some beneficiaries on a portion of their benefits. In addition, Social Security receives income from trust fund investments. Interest income is paid to the trust funds as a credit from the General Fund to the trust funds, in the form of additional non-marketable government securities.

[62] The trust funds' long-term securities have maturities ranging from 1 to 15 years and normally mature in June of each year.

[63] For a detailed discussion, see Social Security Administration, Office of the Chief Actuary, *Social Security Trust Fund Investment Policies and Practices*, Actuarial Note Number 142, January 1999, http://www.ssa.gov/OACT/NOTES/pdf_notes/note142.pdf (hereafter cited as SSA Actuarial Note Number 142).

[64] For SSA's projections of Social Security trust fund operations, see 2010 Annual Report of the Board of Board of Trustees of the Federal Old-Age and Survivors Insurance and Federal Disability Insurance Trust Funds, Washington, DC, August 5, 2010, p. 2, http://www.ssa.gov/OACT/TR/2010/tr2010.pdf. For projections from the Congressional Budget Office (CBO), see Congressional Budget Office, 2010 Long-Term Projections for Social Security: Additional Information, Washington, DC, October 2010, p. 1, http://www.cbo.gov/ftpdocs/119xx/doc11943/10-22- SocialSecurity_chartbook.pdf and The Budget and Economic Outlook: Fiscal Years 2011 to 2021, January 2011, Appendix C. Note that Social Security's cash deficit will be offset by interest income for many years, with the result that Social Security will continue to run a positive total (or "primary") cash flow balance until the trust funds are exhausted in 2037 (under the intermediate projections of the Social Security Board of Trustees) or 2039 (under the projections by CBO). Social Security benefits scheduled under current law can be paid in full as long as there is a positive balance in the trust funds.

[65] P.L. 111-312 makes no change to the Social Security payroll tax rate for employers (6.2%) or to the amount of wages and net self-employment income subject to the Social Security payroll tax ($106,800 in 2011).

[66] See Title VI of H.R. 4853 as passed by the House and the Senate at http://www.gpo.gov/fdsys/pkg/BILLS111hr4853enr/pdf/BILLS-111hr4853enr.pdf.

[67] SSA Actuarial Note Number 142, p. 3.

In: Debt Limit Management...
Editors: J. D. Antonellis, N. P. Barone ISBN: 978-1-61324-418-0


*Chapter 2*

# THE DEBT LIMIT: HISTORY AND RECENT INCREASES*

*D. Andrew Austin and Mindy R. Levit*

## SUMMARY

Total debt of the federal government can increase in two ways. First, debt increases when the government sells debt to the public to finance budget deficits and acquire the financial resources needed to meet its obligations. This increases *debt held by the public*. Second, debt increases when the federal government issues debt to certain government accounts, such as the Social Security, Medicare, and Transportation trust funds, in exchange for their reported surpluses. This increases *debt held by government accounts*. The sum of *debt held by the public* and *debt held by government accounts* is the total federal debt. Surpluses reduce debt held by the public, while deficits raise it. Total federal debt outstanding was $14,104 billion on February 7, 2011. The U.S. Treasury projects the federal debt will reach its statutory limit in April or May 2011, although tax policy, spending changes, and economic trends, could affect that timing. Without a debt limit increase, funding federal operations after the middle of 2011 may be complicated.

A statutory limit has restricted total federal debt since 1917 when Congress passed the Second Liberty Bond Act. Congress has voted to raise the debt limit ten times since 2001. Deficits each year since 2001

---

* This is an edited, reformatted and augmented version of a Congressional Research Services publication, dated February 8, 2011.

and the persistent increases in debt held by government accounts repeatedly raised the debt to or near the limit in place at the time. Congress raised the limit in June 2002, and by December 2002 the U.S. Department of the Treasury asked Congress for another increase, which was passed in May 2003. In June 2004, the Treasury asked for another debt limit increase. After Congress recessed in mid-October 2004 without acting, the Secretary of the Treasury told Congress that the actions he was taking to avoid exceeding the debt limit would suffice only through mid-November. Congress approved a debt limit increase in a post-election session, which the President signed on November 19, 2004. In 2005, reconciliation instructions in the FY2006 budget resolution (H.Con.Res. 95) included a debt limit increase. With no action having been taken by December 2005, the Secretary of the Treasury sent several letters warning Congress that the Treasury would exhaust its options to avoid default by mid-March 2006. Congress passed an increase in mid-March, which the President signed on March 20. The House indirectly approved legislation (H.J.Res. 43) to raise the debt limit by $850 billion to $9,815 billion. The Senate approved the resolution on September 27, 2007, and it was signed by the President two days later.

The current economic slowdown led to sharply higher deficits in recent years, which led to a series of debt limit increases. The Housing and Economic Recovery Act of 2008 (H.R. 3221), signed into law (P.L. 110-289) on July 30, 2008, included a debt limit increase. The Emergency Economic Stabilization Act of 2008 (H.R. 1424), signed into law on October 3 (P.L. 110-343), raised the debt limit again. The debt limit rose a third time in less than a year to $12,104 billion with the passage of American Recovery and Reinvestment Act of 2009 on February 13, 2009 (ARRA; H.R. 1), which was signed into law on February 17, 2009 (P.L. 111-5).

The House's adoption of the conference report on the FY2010 budget resolution (S.Con.Res. 13) on April 29, 2009, triggered the automatic passage of H.J.Res. 45 to raise the debt limit to $13,029 billion. In August 2009, Treasury reportedly said that the debt limit would be reached in mid-October, although it later stated that the limit would not be reached until December 2009. H.R. 4314, passed by the House on December 16, 2009, and by the Senate on December 24, raised the debt limit to $12,394 billion when the President signed the measure (P.L. 111-123) on December 28. On January 28, the Senate passed an amended version of H.J.Res. 45, which the House passed on February 4 and the President signed on February 12 (P.L. 111-139), raising the limit to $14,294 billion. This report, written with the assistance of Joseph McCormack, will be updated as events warrant.

# INTRODUCTION

The statutory debt limit applies to almost all federal debt.[1] The limit applies to federal debt held by the public (that is, debt held outside the federal government itself) and to federal debt held by the government's own accounts. Federal trust funds, such as Social Security, Medicare, Transportation, and Civil Service Retirement accounts, hold most of this internally held debt.[2] The government's surpluses or deficits determine essentially all of the change in debt held by the public.[3] The government's on-budget fiscal balance, which excludes a small U.S. Postal Service net surplus or deficit and a large Social Security surplus of payroll taxes net of paid benefits, does not directly affect debt held in government accounts.[4] Increases or decreases in debt held by government accounts result from net financial flows into accounts holding the debt, such as the Social Security Trust Fund. Legal requirements and government accounting practices also affect levels of debt held by government accounts.[5]

On February 7, 2011, total federal debt outstanding was $14,104 billion, and debt subject to the debt limit was $14,052 billion, about $240 billion below the current statutory debt limit of $14,294 billion.[6] The U.S. Treasury said it will draw down the Supplementary Financing Program (SFP), an initiative intended to help manage monetary policy, from $200 billion to $5 billion, which will provide additional headroom under the limit.[7] Given the size of the FY2011 federal deficit, estimated at $1,480 billion by the Congressional Budget Office (CBO) in January 2011, that additional headroom may not provide substantial additional time before the debt limit nears.[8]

U.S. Treasury estimates that federal debt will reach its limit in April or May 2011.[9] Some Wall Street analysts have been expecting federal debt to near its limit in that time frame, although many factors, including federal tax policy and strength of the economic recovery, could affect federal debt trends.[10] On January 6, 2011, Treasury Secretary Geithner sent a letter to Senate Majority Leader Harry Reid requesting an increase in the debt limit. At that time, Secretary Geithner stated that federal debt limit would likely reach its statutory limit between March 31 and May 16, 2011.[11] Without a debt limit increase, the U.S. Treasury may face difficulty in funding federal operations after the middle of 2011.

# THE DEBT LIMIT AND THE TREASURY

Standard methods of financing federal activities or meeting government obligations used by the U.S. Department of Treasury (Treasury) can be hobbled when federal debt nears its legal limit. The government's income and outlays vary over the course of the year, producing monthly surpluses and deficits that affect the level of debt, whether or not the government has a surplus or deficit for the entire year. The government accounts holding federal debt also can experience monthly deficits and surpluses, even for the major accounts that usually show annual surpluses. The ability to borrow is a central to Treasury cash management systems that handle fluctuations in federal revenues and outlays. When federal debt has neared the debt limit in the past, limiting the U.S. Treasury's borrowing authority, financial management has become more complicated.

If the U.S. Treasury were precluded from borrowing due to a binding debt limit in times when federal outlays outpaced revenues, the government would no longer meet all of its legal obligations in a timely manner.[12] If the limit prevents the Treasury from issuing new debt to manage short-term cash flows or to finance an annual deficit, the government may be unable to obtain the cash needed to pay its bills or it may be unable to invest the surpluses of designated government accounts (federal trust funds) in federal debt as generally required by law. In either case, the Treasury is left in a bind; the law requires that the government's legal obligations be paid, but the debt limit may prevent it from issuing the debt that would allow it to do so on time.

Among other consequences, a sustained inability to pay obligations on time could hinder the U.S. Treasury's ability to borrow on advantageous terms in the future. A delay in interest payments on Treasury securities would trigger a default and risk serious negative repercussions for economies and financial markets around the world. Default might be avoided in such situations by delaying other types of federal payments and transfers. A government that delays payment of an obligation, in effect, borrows from vendors, contractors, beneficiaries, state and local governments, or employees who are not paid on time. In some cases, delaying payments incurs interest penalties under some statutes such as the Prompt Payment Act, which directs the government to pay interest penalties to contractors if it does not pay them by the required payment date,[13] and the Internal Revenue Code, which requires the government to pay interest penalties if tax refunds are delayed beyond a certain date.[14]

Past Treasury Secretaries, when faced with a nearly binding debt ceiling, have used special strategies to handle cash and debt management responsibilities. Actions taken in the past include suspending sales of nonmarketable debt, postponing or downsizing marketable debt auctions, and withholding receipts that would be transferred to certain government trust funds. Congress has authorized the Treasury Secretary to invoke a "debt issuance suspension period" to use some of these strategies using the Civil Service Retirement Fund and the Thrift Savings Fund, along with the authority to make those funds whole after an easing of the debt constraint.[15]

Some U.S. Treasury responses to the credit crunch that began in mid 2007 created balance sheet items that might expand options available to the Treasury Secretary. The U.S. Treasury, however, is unlikely to maintain smooth debt management operations indefinitely in the face of a continuing imbalance between federal revenues and outlays without an increase in the debt limit.

## Why Have a Debt Limit?

The debt limit can hinder the Treasury's ability to manage the federal government's finances, as noted above. In extreme cases, when the federal debt is very near its statutory limit, the Treasury must take unusual and extraordinary measures to meet federal obligations.[16] While the debt limit has never caused the federal government to default on its obligations, it has at times caused great inconvenience and has added uncertainty to Treasury operations.

The debt limit also provides Congress with the strings to control the federal purse, allowing Congress to assert its constitutional prerogatives to control spending.[17] The debt limit also imposes a form of fiscal accountability that compels Congress and the President to take visible action to allow further federal borrowing when the federal government spends more than it collects in revenues. In the words of one author, the debt limit "expresses a national devotion to the idea of thrift and to economical management of the fiscal affairs of the government."[18] On the other hand, some budget experts have advocated elimination of the debt limit, arguing that other controls provided by the modern congressional budget process established in 1974 have superseded the debt limit, and that the limit does little to alter spending and revenue policies that determine the size of the federal deficit.[19]

# A BRIEF HISTORY OF THE FEDERAL DEBT LIMIT

## Origins of the Federal Debt Limit

The statutory limit on federal debt began with the Second Liberty Bond Act of 1917,[20] which helped finance the United States' entry into World War I.[21] By allowing the Treasury to issue long-term Liberty Bonds, which were marketed to the public at large, the federal government held down its interest costs.[22]

Before World War I, Congress often authorized specific loans, such as the Panama Canal loan, or allowed the Treasury to issue specific types of debt instruments, such as certificates of indebtedness, bills, notes and bonds.[23] In other cases, especially in time of war, Congress provided the Treasury with discretion, subject to broad limits, to choose debt instruments.[24] For example, the 1898 War Revenue Act (30 Stat. 448-470) that funded Spanish-American War costs granted the Treasury Secretary the authority to issue $100 million in certificates of indebtedness with maturities under a year and $400 million in longer term notes and bonds.[25] Proponents of the Act made clear their intention to allow the Treasury Secretary substantial administrative leeway.[26]

With the passage of the Second Liberty Bond Act, Congress enacted aggregate constraints on certificates of indebtedness and on bonds that allowed the Treasury greater ability to respond to changing conditions and more flexibility in financial management. Debt limit legislation in the following two decades also set separate limits for different categories of debt, such as bills, certificates, and bonds.

In 1939, Congress eliminated separate limits on bonds and on other types of debt, which created the first aggregate limit that covered nearly all public debt.[27] This measure gave the Treasury freer rein to manage the federal debt as it saw fit. Thus, the Treasury could issue debt instruments with maturities that would reduce interest costs and minimize financial risks stemming from future interest rate changes.[28] On the other hand, although the Treasury was delegated greater independence of action, the debt limit on the eve of World War II was much closer to total federal debt than it had been at the end of World War I. For example, the 1919 Victory Liberty Bond Act (P.L. 65-328) raised the maximum allowable federal debt to $43 billion, far above the $25.5 billion in total federal debt at the end of FY1919.[29] By contrast, the debt limit in 1939 was $45 billion, only about 10% above the $40.4 billion total federal debt of that time.

## World War II and after

The debt ceiling was raised to accommodate accumulating costs for World War II in each year from 1941 through 1945, when it was set at $300 billion.[30] After World War II ended, the debt limit was reduced to $275 billion. Because the Korean War was mostly financed by higher taxes rather than by increased debt, the limit remained at $275 billion until 1954. After 1954, the debt limit was reduced twice and increased seven times, until March 1962 when it again reached $300 billion, its level at the end of World War II. Since March 1962, Congress has enacted 74 separate measures that have altered the limit on federal debt.[31] Most of these changes in the debt limit were, measured in percentage terms, small in comparison to changes adopted in wartime or during the Great Depression. Some recent increases in the debt limit, however, were large in dollar terms. For instance, in May 2003, the debt limit increased by $984 billion.

# THE DEBT CEILING IN THE LAST DECADE

During the four years (FY1998-FY2001) the government ran surpluses, federal debt held by intergovernmental accounts grew by $855 billion and debt held by the public fell by almost $450 billion. Since FY2001, however, debt held by the public has grown due to persistent and substantial budget deficits. Debt held in government accounts also has grown, in large part because Social Security payroll taxes have exceeded payments of beneficiaries. **Table 1** shows components of debt in current dollars and as percentages of gross domestic product (GDP).[32]

**Figure 1** shows the components of federal debt as shares of gross domestic product (GDP) from FY1940 through FY2010.[33] Federal debt held by government accounts has grown steadily since 1980. Debt held by the public, which changes in response to total surpluses or deficits, grew as a share of GDP through the mid-1990s. After FY1992, deficits shrank, and from FY1998 through FY2001 the federal government ran surpluses.[34] Those surpluses, along with rapid GDP growth, reduced debt held by the public as a percentage of GDP. When large deficits returned and GDP growth slowed in the early 2000s, debt held by the public as a share of GDP again increased.

Smaller deficits in FY2006 and FY2007 led to smaller increases in publicly held debt. The total FY2007 deficit fell to 1.2% of GDP according to CBO.[35] Financial turmoil in 2007 and 2008 and a subsequent recession that began in late 2007 led to federal actions taken to stabilize the housing and financial markets. The recession reduced federal revenues and increased federal spending, leading to large deficits and a series of debt limit increases.

## The Debt Limit Issue in 2002

Accumulating debt in government accounts produced most of the pressure on the debt limit that occurred early in 2002. As deficits reemerged in FY2002, increases in debt held by the public added to the pressure on the debt limit in the spring of 2002. During the four fiscal years with surpluses (FY1998-FY2001), the increases in federally held debt and decreases in debt held by the public produced a net increase of $405 billion in total debt subject to limit. At the beginning of FY2002 (October 1, 2001), debt subject to limit was within $217 billion of the existing $5,950 billion debt limit.[36] Between then and the end of May 2002, debt subject to limit increased by another $217 billion, divided between a $117 billion increase in debt held by government accounts and a $100 billion increase in debt held by the public, putting the debt close to the $5,950 billion limit. **Table A-1**, presented in the **Appendix**, shows month-by-month debt totals and accumulations from September 2001 through December 2010.

In the fall of 2001, the Administration recognized that a deteriorating budget outlook and continued growth in debt held by government accounts were likely to lead to the debt limit soon being reached. In early December 2001, it asked Congress to raise the debt limit by $750 billion to $6,700 billion. As the debt moved closer to and reached the debt limit over the first six months of FY2002, the Administration asked Congress repeatedly to increase the debt limit, warning of adverse financial consequences were the limit not raised.

On April 4, 2002, the Treasury held debt below the limit by invoking its legislatively mandated authority to suspend reinvestment of government securities in the G-Fund of the federal employees' Thrift Savings Plan (TSP). This allowed the Treasury to issue new debt and meet the government's obligations. On April 15, debt subject to limit stood at $5,949,975 million, just $25 million below the limit. Once April 15 tax revenues flowed in, the Treasury "made whole" the G-Fund by restoring all of the debt that had not been issued to the TSP over this period and crediting the fund with interest it would have earned on that debt.[37] By the end of April, debt subject to limit had fallen back $35 billion below the limit.

**Table 1. Components of Debt Subject to Limit, FY1996-FY2010 (in billions of current dollars and as percentage of GDP)**

| | | Debt Subject to Limit | | | | | |
|---|---|---|---|---|---|---|---|
| | | Total | | Held by Government Accounts | | Held by the Public | |
| End of Fiscal Year | Debt Limit | $ Billion | % of GDP | $ Billion | % of GDP | $ Billion | % of GDP |
| 1996 | $5,500 | $5,137.2 | 65.7% | 1,432.4 | 18.3% | 3,704.8 | 47.4% |
| 1997 | 5,950 | 5,327.6 | 64.2 | 1,581.9 | 19.0 | 3,745.8 | 45.1 |
| 1998 | 5,950 | 5,439.4 | 62.2 | 1,742.1 | 19.9 | 3,697.4 | 42.3 |
| 1999 | 5,950 | 5,567.7 | 60.1 | 1,958.2 | 21.1 | 3,609.5 | 38.9 |
| 2000 | 5,950 | 5,591.6 | 57.0 | 2,203.9 | 22.4 | 3,387.7 | 34.5 |
| 2001 | 5,950 | 5,732.8 | 56.6 | 2,436.5 | 24.1 | 3,296.3 | 32.5 |
| 2002 | 6,400 | 6,161.4 | 58.9 | 2,644.2 | 25.3 | 3,517.2 | 33.6 |
| 2003 | 7,384 | 6,737.6 | 61.4 | 2,846.7 | 25.9 | 3,890.8 | 35.5 |
| 2004 | 7,384 | 7,333.4 | 62.5 | 3,056.6 | 26.0 | 4,276.8 | 36.4 |
| 2005 | 8,184 | 7,871.0 | 64.0 | 3,301.0 | 26.9 | 4,570.1 | 37.2 |
| 2006 | 8,965 | 8,420.3 | 64.2 | 3,610.4 | 27.5 | 4,809.8 | 36.7 |
| 2007 | 9,815[a] | 8,921.3 | 65.4 | 3,903.7 | 28.6 | 5,017.6 | 36.8 |
| 2008 | 10,615[b] | 9,960.0 | 70.0 | 4,180.0 | 29.4 | 5,780.3 | 40.6 |
| 2009 | 12,104[c] | 11,909.8 | 84.1 | 4,358.0 | 30.8 | 7,551.9 | 53.3 |

## Table 1. Components

| | | Debt Subject to Limit | | | | | |
|---|---|---|---|---|---|---|---|
| | | Total | | Held by Government Accounts | | Held by the Public | |
| End of Fiscal Year | Debt Limit | $ Billion | % of GDP | $ Billion | % of GDP | $ Billion | % of GDP |
| 2010 | 14,294[d] | 13,510.8 | 92.1 | 4,585.7 | 31.3 | 9,022.8 | 61.5 |
| Change during FY1998 - FY2001 | $405.2 | | $854.6 | | | $-449.5 | |
| Change during FY2002 - FY2010 | $7,778.0 | | $2,073.1 | | | $5,704.9 | |

Source: U.S. Department of the Treasury, Financial Management Service, *Treasury Bulletin*, June 2001 and December 2006. Bureau of the Public Debt, *Monthly Statement of Public Debt*, various issues. CRS calculations.

Notes: For the fiscal years 1996 through 2000, the amounts held by government accounts and held by the public are approximations. In 2001, the Treasury publications began distinguishing holders of debt subject to limit. The numbers in the table showing this breakdown for FY1996 through FY2000 were calculated by subtracting debts of the Federal Financing Bank, an arm of the Treasury whose debt is not subject to limit, from total debt held by government accounts. This calculation approximates the amount of that debt subject to limit. This approximation overestimates debt by billions of dollars because estimates of unamortized discount are unavailable. This adjusted amount was then subtracted from total debt subject to limit to produce an approximate measure of debt held by the public subject to limit. Because the amount held by government accounts is overestimated, the resulting measure of debt held by the public subject to limit is underestimated. Totals may not sum due to rounding.

a. Debt limit increased September 29, 2007, to $9,815 billion.

b. The debt limit was increased twice in 2008—to $10,615 billion on July 30 and then to $11,315 billion on October 3, at the start of FY2009.

c. Debt limit was increased February 17, 2009, to $12,104 billion.

d. Debt limit was increased February 12, 2010, to $14,294 billion.

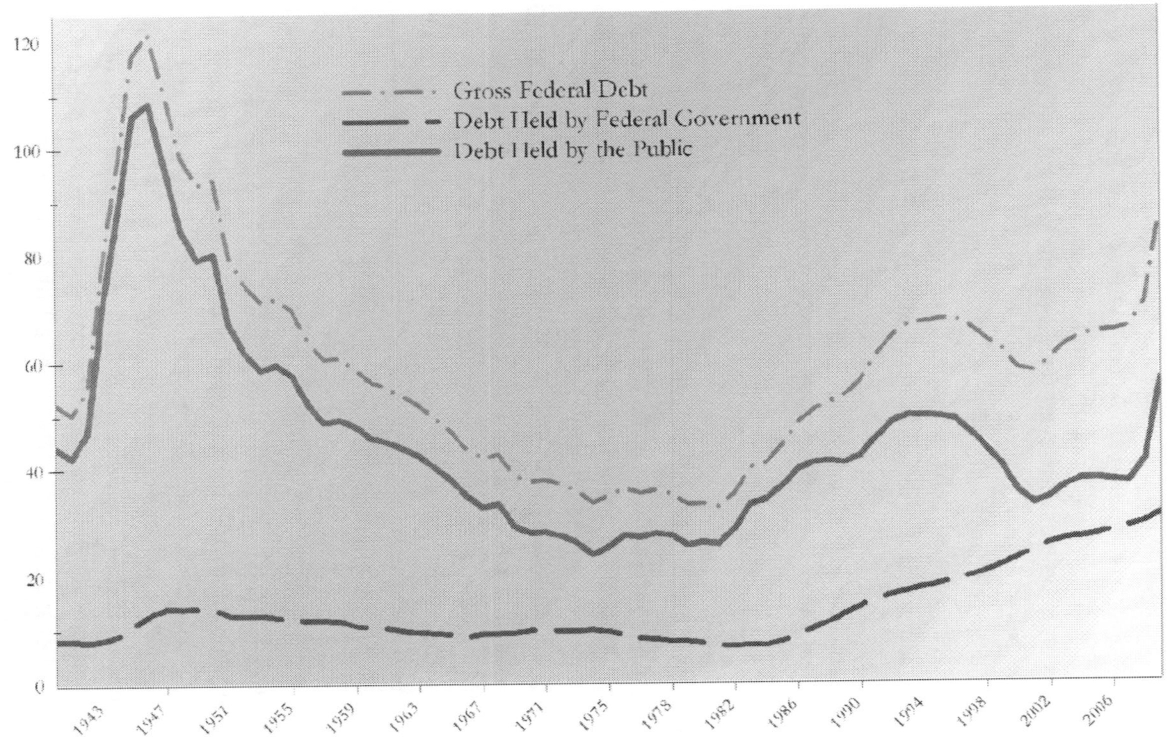


Source: OMB, Budget of the United States for FY2010, Historical Tables, February 2009; Mid-Session Review, August 2009.

Figure 1. Components of Federal Debt As a Percentage of GDP, FY1940-FY2009.

### *Resolving the Debt Limit Issue in 2002*

By the middle of May 2002, debt subject to limit had again risen to within $15 million of the statutory limit. At the FY2002 average spending rate, $15 million equaled about five minutes of federal outlays. The Treasury, for the second time in 2002, used its statutory authority to avoid a default. The Treasury's financing problems, however, would persist without an increase in the debt limit. On May 14, the Treasury asked Congress to raise the debt limit or enact other statutory changes allowing the Treasury to issue new debt. A Treasury news release stated "absent extraordinary actions, the government will exceed the statutory debt ceiling no later than May 16," and that

> a "debt issuance suspension period" will begin no later than May 16 [2002].... [This] allows the Treasury to suspend or redeem investments in two trust funds, which will provide flexibility to fund the operations of the government during this period.[38]

The Treasury reduced federal debt held by these government accounts by replacing it with noninterest-bearing, non-debt instruments, which enabled it to issue new debt to meet the government's obligations. The Treasury claimed these extraordinary actions would suffice, at the latest, through June 28, 2002. Without a debt limit increase by that date, the Treasury indicated it would need to take other actions to avoid breaching the ceiling. By June 21, the Treasury had postponed a regular securities auction, but took no other actions. With large payments and other obligations due at the end of June and at the beginning of July, the Treasury stated it would soon exhaust all options to issue debt and fulfill government obligations, putting the government on the verge of a default.

During May and June 2002, Congress took steps to increase the debt limit. The FY2002 supplemental appropriations bill (H.R. 4775) passed by the House on May 24 included, after extended debate, language allowing any eventual House-Senate conference on the legislation to increase the debt limit. However, the Senate's supplemental appropriations bill (S. 2551; incorporated as an amendment to H.R. 4775, June 3, 2002) omitted debt-limit-increasing language. The Senate leadership expressed strong reluctance to include a debt limit increase in the supplemental appropriation bill. Instead, on June 11, the Senate adopted a bill (S. 2578), without debate, to raise the debt limit by $450 billion to $6,400 billion. At that time, a $450 billion debt limit increase was thought to provide enough borrowing authority for government operations through the rest of calendar year 2002, if not through the summer of 2003.

With the possibility of default looming over it, the House passed the $450 billion debt limit increase by a single vote on June 27. The President signed the bill into law on June 28 (P.L. 107-199, 116 Stat. 734), ending the 2002 debt limit crisis.[39]

## The Debt Limit Issue in 2003

On Christmas Eve, 2002, Kenneth Dam, Deputy Secretary of the Treasury sent a letter to Congress requesting an unspecified increase in the debt limit by late February 2003, signaling that the $6,400 billion debt limit would then be reached.[40] The 108th Congress, still in the process of organizing itself, did not immediately respond. Through the winter and into the spring, the Treasury repeatedly requested that the debt limit be raised to avoid serious financial problems. By February 20, 2003, the Treasury, as in 2002, used legislatively mandated measures to manage debt holdings of certain government accounts to avoid reaching the debt limit. These actions included the replacement of internally held government debt with non-debt instruments in certain government accounts and not issuing new debt to these accounts. These actions allowed the Treasury to issue additional debt to the public to acquire the cash needed to pay for the government's commitments or to issue new debt to other federal accounts.

Through the rest of February and into May, the Treasury held debt subject to limit $15 million below the debt ceiling.[41] The adoption of the conference report on the FY2004 budget resolution (H.Con.Res. 95; H.Rept. 108-71) on April 11, 2003, in the House triggered the "Gephardt rule" (House Rule XXVII) that deems to have passed legislation (in this case, H.J.Res. 51) raising the debt limit to accommodate the spending and revenue levels approved in the adopted budget resolution.[42]

The Senate received the debt-limit legislation on April 11, but did not act until May 23, after receiving further Treasury warnings of imminent default. On that day, debt subject to limit was $25 million (or 0.0004%) below the existing $6,400 billion limit. The Senate adopted the legislation, after rejecting eight amendments and sent it to the President, who signed it on May 27. This legislation raised the debt limit to $7,384 billion (P.L. 108-24, 117 Stat. 710).

## The Debt Limit Issue in 2004

In January 2004, CBO estimated that the debt limit, then set at $7,384 billion, would be reached the following summer.[43] In June 2004, the Treasury asked Congress to raise the debt limit in order to avoid the disruptions to government finances experienced in the previous two years.[44] In August, and again in September, the Treasury declared that the debt limit would be reached in the first half of October. On October 14, debt subject to limit reached $7,383,975 million, just $25 million below the existing limit. The Treasury employed methods used in the previous two years to keep debt under the legal limit. On October 14, Secretary of the Treasury John Snow informed Congress, just before the election recess, that available measures to avoid breaching the debt limit would be exhausted by mid-November.[45] Without an increase in the debt limit, the Treasury would be unable to meet all of the government's existing obligations, which could undermine the U.S. government's reputation in capital markets and raise costs of federal borrowing.

Although the House passed a budget resolution for FY2005 in the spring of 2004, it did not reach final agreement with the Senate on the measure. Without a budget resolution passed by Congress, no resolution to raise the debt limit could be deemed passed by the House automatically under the Gephardt rule. Consequently, no measure was available to send to the Senate. As the debt approached the limit through the summer and into the fall, no legislation was moved to raise the debt limit.

Earlier, in September 2004, the House had added an amendment to the FY2005 Transportation-Treasury appropriations (H.R. 5025) in an effort to remove the Treasury's flexibility in financing the government as federal debt approached and reached the existing limit. Without that flexibility, the government would be unable to meet its financial obligations as the amount of debt neared the limit. The legislation cleared the House, but the Senate did not act on it.

After the elections, Senator Frist, on November 16, 2004, introduced legislation (S. 2986) to raise the debt limit by $800 billion, from $7,384 billion to $8,184 billion. The Senate approved the increase on November 17, 2004. The House considered and approved the increase on November 18. The President signed the legislation into law (P.L. 108-415, 118 Stat. 2337) on November 19, 2004. Estimates made at that time anticipated the new limit would be reached between August and December 2005.

Shortly before the increase in the debt limit, the Treasury delayed a debt auction and informed Congress that it would invoke a "debt limit suspension period" as it had in previous years. The increase in the debt limit in mid-November allowed the Treasury to reschedule the debt auction and cancel, before it began, the "debt limit suspension period."

## The Debt Limit Issue in 2005, 2006, and 2007

Debt limit increases in 2005, 2006, and 2007 took a less dramatic path than those in President Bush's first term. In 2005, Congress included three reconciliation instructions in the FY2006 budget resolution (H.Con.Res. 95, 109th Congress; April 28, 2005), the third of which directed the House Committee on Ways and Means and the Senate Finance Committee to report bills raising the debt limit. The instructions specified a $781 billion debt limit increase, to $8,965 billion, with a reporting date of no later than September 30, 2005. Neither committee reported a bill to raise the debt limit.

The adoption of the conference report on the FY2006 budget resolution in late April 2005 also triggered the Gephardt rule (House Rule XXVII), producing a House Joint Resolution (H.J.Res. 47) that also would raise the debt limit by $781 billion to $8,965 billion. Under the rule, the resolution was automatically deemed passed by the House and sent to the Senate. Through the end of the first session of the 109th Congress, the Senate had not considered H.J.Res. 47, nor had Congress considered a reconciliation bill raising the debt limit as called for in the budget resolution.

At the end of December 2005, Secretary of the Treasury Snow wrote Congress that the debt limit would probably be reached in mid-February 2006, although the Treasury could take actions that maintain the debt below its limit until mid-March. He therefore requested an increase in the debt limit.[46] In two more letters, sent on February 19 and March 6, Secretary Snow advised Congress that the Treasury was taking measures within its legal discretion to avoid reaching the limit and that these measures would suffice only until the middle of March 2006. Secretary Snow authorized actions used previously by the Treasury, including declaring a debt issuance suspension period. As March began, the government was again close to becoming unable to meet its obligations. During the week of March 13 the Senate took up H.J.Res. 47. On March 16, the Senate passed a debt limit increase after rejecting several amendments. The President's signature on March 20, 2006, then raised the debt limit (P.L. 109-182) to $8,965 billion.

In mid-May 2007, Congress passed the conference report (H.Rept. 110-153) on the FY2008 budget resolution. The House's Gephardt rule, triggered by the adoption of the conference report on the budget resolution, resulted in the automatic engrossment of a joint resolution (in this case, H.J.Res. 43, 110$^{th}$ Congress) raising the debt limit by $850 billion to $9,815 billion, and sending it to the Senate. At the end of July 2007, the Treasury asked Congress to raise the debt limit, stating the limit would be reached in early October 2007. In August, the CBO Director said that projections suggested that the limit would be reached in late October or early November. Without an increase, the Treasury indicated that it would take steps within its legal authority to avoid exceeding the debt limit. The Senate Finance Committee approved the House resolution (H.J.Res. 43) without changes on September 12, 2007. The Senate then passed the measure on September 27, which the President signed on September 29, 2007 (P.L. 110-91).

## The Economic Slowdown and Federal Debt

### *Fiscal Policy Considerations*

The U.S. economy is currently recovering slowly from a severe economic recession that began in December 2007 and ended in June 2009.[47] The economic slowdown began with a rapid deceleration of housing prices and a rise in interest rate spreads between private lending rates and benchmark Federal Reserve rates, indicating an increasing reluctance of major financial institutions to lend to each other as well as to firms and individuals. This led to sharply higher federal deficit spending in FY2008 spurred by several major actions taken by Congress to unfreeze credit markets, boost consumption, and increase spending. Deficit spending was even higher in FY2009, with higher than average deficits as a percentage of GDP persisting into the next decade, likely leading to further increases in the federal debt and debt limit. While deficits for FY2010 were slightly lower and fiscal conditions are projected to improve in FY2011, deficits remain high relative to historical experience.

Economic recession affects the federal deficit in several ways. First, falling prices of many assets and equities can sharply reduce federal revenues from capital gains taxes and from the corporate tax. Second, individual income taxes, the largest component of federal revenues, may also fall if jobs are cut and unemployment increases due to economic conditions. Third, "automatic stabilizers" such as unemployment insurance and income support programs pay out more money as unemployment rises and the number of households eligible for means-tested benefits rises, thus increasing federal spending.

Boosting the economy through deficit spending provides a fiscal stimulus if the output levels of goods and services produced in the nation are below their potential levels. Deficit spending, however, can help accelerate inflation if output levels are near or at potential levels, and in addition, exacerbates long-term fiscal challenges. Several economists have expressed concerns that inflation, which had been relatively low since the early 1980s, could accelerate due to rising prices of food, energy, and primary commodities. While inflation would reduce the market value of the federal deficit, it would require Treasury to pay higher nominal interest rates on federal debt. The U.S. economy, however, is currently operating well below its potential, which has kept inflation at lower levels.

### *Raising the Debt Ceiling in 2008, 2009, and 2010*

In a March 2008 report, CBO estimated the President's budget would lead to a $396 billion deficit in FY2008 and a $342 billion deficit in FY2009.[48] The actual deficit for FY2008 reached $455 billion. In August 2009, CBO estimated the deficit would total $1,587 billion in FY2009 and $1,381 billion in FY2010.[49] As a result of the current economic conditions and the actions of the federal government to bring the economy out of recession, the federal debt limit was raised twice in the second half of 2008 and twice in 2009.

The House Concurrent Resolution on the Budget (H.Con.Res. 312) recommended policies that would result in a $10,200 billion debt in FY2009. The Senate Concurrent Resolution on the Budget S.Con.Res. 70) recommended policies that would result in a total debt of $10,278 billion in FY2009.[50] Implementing either set of policies would require an increase in the federal debt limit. The conference agreement (H.Rept. 110-659) also recommended spending levels that would lead to a debt subject to limit of $10,207 billion in FY2009, a level that would require an increase in the statutory debt limit. The budget conference report passed the Senate on a 48-45 vote on June 4, 2008. The House passed the measure on the next day by a 214-210 vote. Agreement on the FY2009 budget resolution automatically created and deemed passed in the House legislation (H.J.Res. 92) that would increase the debt limit from its current level of $9,815 billion to $10,615 billion. Because the Senate did not take up H.J.Res. 92, the debt limit remained at $9,815 billion.

Subsequently, the House passed an amended version of the Housing and Economic Recovery Act of 2008 (H.R. 3221) by a vote of 272-152 that included a debt limit increase to $10,615 billion on July 23, 2008. The Senate then passed the measure on July 26 on a 72-13 vote. The President signed the bill on July 30 (P.L. 110-289), increasing the debt limit. In addition to increasing the debt limit, the act also contained provisions that would temporarily authorize the Secretary of Treasury to extend a line of credit to mortgage guarantee agencies Freddie Mac and Fannie Mae. The act also created the a new independent agency called the Federal Housing Finance Agency (FHFA), which replaced the Department of Housing and Urban Development Office of Federal Housing Enterprise Oversight (OFHEO) and the Federal Housing Finance Board (FHFB).

While CBO indicated that it was more likely than not that such intervention would not be needed, it also estimated a 5% chance of a cost to taxpayers of more than $100 billion.[51] Because debt subject to limit was just $339 billion less than the debt ceiling of $9,815 billion when the Senate passed H.R. 3221, some financial market participants may have worried that the debt limit, without an increase, might have hindered the Treasury Secretary's ability to intervene to support Freddie Mac and Fannie Mae. On September 7, 2008, the FHFA placed Fannie Mae and Freddie Mac in conservatorship, providing FHFA with the full powers to control the assets and operations of the firms.

Since the deprivatization of Fannie Mae and Freddie Mac, the federal government has acted to provide stability to financial markets.[52] On September 20, 2008, the U.S. Treasury submitted a proposal to Congress to authorize the Treasury Secretary to buy mortgage-related assets in order to stabilize financial markets. The Treasury proposal would allow Treasury holdings of mortgage-related securities up to $700 billion and would raise the debt limit to $11,315 billion.[53]

Representative Barney Frank proposed an amendment (Emergency Economic Stabilization Act of 2008) to a vehicle measure (H.R. 3997) that incorporated the main tenets of the Treasury proposal including raising the debt limit to $11,315 billion.[54] On September 29, 2008, however, the House rejected that amendment.

On October 1, 2008, the Senate voted on, and passed, a different version of the Emergency Economic Stabilization Act of 2008 (H.R. 1424) that included the same debt limit increase.[55] The House passed H.R. 1424 on October 3, 2008, and it was signed into law by the President (P.L. 110-343) on the same day, raising the debt limit to $11,315 billion.

Current economic conditions led Congress to consider another economic stimulus measure. This measure contains both tax cuts and spending increases, which will increase the deficit by reducing revenues and increasing outlays. The American Recovery and Reinvestment Act of 2009 (ARRA) as passed by the Senate on February 10, 2009 (Division B of the Senate Substitute amendment to H.R. 1 and S. 350), contained a provision which would raise the debt limit to $12,140 billion. The version of this legislation originally passed by the House omitted this provision. The final conference agreement on ARRA was passed by the House and Senate on February 13, 2009, and signed by the President on February 17, 2009 (P.L. 111-5). This measure contained a provision increasing the debt limit to $12,104 billion.

The conference report on the Concurrent Resolution on the Budget for FY2010 (S.Con.Res. 13) recommended policies that would lead to a debt subject to limit of $13,233 billion in FY2010, a level that would require an increase in the statutory debt limit. The budget resolution also contained a revised estimate of debt subject to limit of $12,016 billion for FY2009. The adoption of this conference report on April 29, 2009, triggered the Gephardt rule (House Rule XXVII), producing a House Joint Resolution (H.J.Res. 45) that would raise the debt limit by $925 billion to $13,029 billion. Under the rule, the resolution was automatically deemed passed by the House and sent to the Senate.

In August 2009, according to media reports, Secretary of Treasury Timothy Geithner notified Congress that the debt limit would be reached in mid-October.[56] On November 4, the U.S. Treasury announced that it could postpone the time when federal debt would reach its statutory limit until the middle or the end of December. [57] Treasury dropped nearly $185 billion from its balance sheet by reducing the amount of loans available through the Supplemental Financing Program, an emergency loan program created in the days following Lehman Brothers' bankruptcy, from $200 billion to $15 billion, which extended the time until the debt limit would be reached.[58] According to media reports, the Obama Administration also contemplated scaling back the Troubled Asset Relief Program (TARP), which could also lower federal debt subject to statutory limit. Repayments of TARP funds by major financial institutions could also lower the amount of debt subject to limit.[59] Other measures, such as those taken in 2003 during a "debt issuance suspension period" (described above), could also have extended the U.S. Treasury's ability to operate within the debt limit. On the other hand, the U.S.

**Table 2** summarizes the increases in the debt limit since 1993.[68]

**Table 2. Increases in the Debt Limit Since 1993**

| Date | Public Law (P.L.) Number | New Debt Limit ($ billion) | Change From Previous Limit ($ billion) |
|---|---|---|---|
| April 6, 1993 | P.L. 103-12 | $4,370[a] | $225 |
| August 10, 1993 | P.L. 103-33 | 4,900 | 530 |
| February 8, 1996 | P.L. 104-103 | ([b]) | — |
| March 12, 1996 | P.L. 104-115 | ([c]) | — |
| March 29, 1996 | P.L. 104-121 | 5,500 | 600[d] |
| August 5, 1997 | P.L. 105-33 | 5,950 | 450 |
| June 28, 2002 | P.L. 107-199 | 6,400 | 450 |
| May 27, 2003 | P.L. 108-24 | 7,384 | 984 |
| Nov. 19, 2004 | P.L. 108-415 | 8,184 | 800 |
| Mar. 20, 2006 | P.L. 109-182 | 8,965 | 781 |
| Sept. 29, 2007 | P.L. 110-91 | 9,815 | 850 |
| July 30, 2008 | P.L. 110-289 | 10,615 | 800 |
| Oct. 3, 2008 | P.L. 110-343 | 11,315 | 700 |
| Feb. 17, 2009 | P.L. 111-5 | 12,104 | 789 |
| Dec. 28, 2009 | P.L. 111-123 | 12,394 | 290 |
| February 12, 2010 | P.L. 111-139 | 14,294 | 1,900 |

Source: CRS, compiled using the Legislative Information System, available at httpi/www.congress; OMB.

[a] Increased the debt limit temporarily through September 30, 1993.

[b] Temporarily exempted from limit obligations in an amount equal to the monthly insurance benefits payable under Title II of the Social Security Act in March 1996, the exemption to expire on the earlier of an increase in the limit or March 15, 1996.

[c] Temporarily exempted from limit (a) obligations in an amount equal to the monthly insurance benefits payable under Title II of the Social Security Act in March 1996 and (b) certain obligations issued to trust funds and other Federal Government accounts, both exemptions to expire on the earlier of an increase in the limit or March 30, 1996.

[d] Difference from debt limit set on August 10, 1983.

Treasury was scheduled to issue $48 billion of nonmarketable securities to the FDIC on December 30 and to make interest payments to various federal trust funds on December 31 totaling about $100 billion, according to Wall Street analysts, which in the absence of a debt limit increase, could have challenged Treasury's debt management activities in the absence of special accounting measures.[60]

In mid-December, according to media reports, senior Members of the House chose to forgo a larger increase in the debt limit in favor of a smaller increase in the debt limit that would allow the U.S. Treasury Department to continue normal debt management operations for two months or so.[61] H.R. 4314, a measure to raise the debt limit to $12,394 billion, was introduced on December 15, 2009, and passed by the House the next day on a 218-214 vote. The Senate passed it on December 24 by a 60-39 vote, and the President signed the measure on December 28. On January 28, the Senate passed an amended version of H.J.Res. 45 on a 60-39 vote. The measure would raise the debt ceiling by $1,900 billion, to $14,294 billion.[62] In addition, one amendment to impose certain pay-as-you-go (PAYGO) restrictions was approved on a 60-40 vote.[63]

Some Members of Congress have called for the creation of a national commission to address federal debt and the government's fiscal situation, which could be enabled through a measure linked to an increase in the debt limit.[64] An amendment (S.Amdt. 3302 to S.Amdt. 3299) to H.J.Res. 45 that would have established a "Bipartisan Task Force for Responsible Fiscal Action" was not approved on a 53-46 vote, having failed to reach 60 votes, on January 26, 2010. President Obama then charged a National Commission on Fiscal Responsibility and Reform (Fiscal Commission) with identifying "policies to improve the fiscal situation in the medium term and to achieve fiscal sustainability over the long run."[65] The Fiscal Commission issued a report on December 1, 2010, and several commissioners issued their own fiscal proposals as well.[66]

The House approved H.J.Res. 45 on a 233-187 vote on February 4, forwarding the measure to the President. The Obama Administration had previously voiced its strong support for a debt limit increase.[67] The President signed the measure (P.L. 111-139) on February 12, 2010.

### *Deficit Estimates*

The size of the debt may remain a concern in the future due to the size of impending federal deficits necessitating further increases in the debt limit.

CBO warns that the current trajectory of federal borrowing is unsustainable and could lead to slower economic growth in the long run as debt rises as a percentage of GDP. The total federal deficit rose from $455 billion in FY2008 to $1,413 billion in FY2009, and is estimated to reach $1,342 billion in FY2010.[69] Much of the increase in deficits can be attributed to weak economic and financial market turmoil that started in late 2007, as well as to federal responses. Nonetheless, many budget experts remain concerned that a slow economic recovery or a "double-dip" recession could keep federal revenues below previous trendline projections for several years, and that the federal government would continue to run large deficits.

## CONCLUDING COMMENTS

Since the late 1950s, the federal government increased its borrowing from the public in all years, except in FY1969 following imposition of a war surcharge and in the period FY1997-FY2001. The persistence of federal budget deficits has required the government to issue more and more debt to the public.[70] The accumulation of Social Security and other trust funds, particularly after 1983 when recommendations of the Greenspan Commission were implemented, led to sustained growth in government-held debt subject to limit.[71] The growth in federal debt held by the public and in intergovernmental accounts, such as trust funds, has periodically obliged Congress to raise the debt limit.

Between August 1997, when the debt limit was raised to $5,950 billion, and the beginning of FY2002 in October 2001, federal budget surpluses reduced debt held by the public. From the end of FY2001, the last fiscal year with a surplus, until the end of FY2008, debt held by the public subject to limit grew by $2,484 billion. Federal debt held in intergovernmental accounts grew steadily throughout the period, rising by $1,743 billion since the beginning of FY2002.

In early 2001, the 10-year budget forecasts projected large and growing surpluses, indicating rapid reduction in debt held by the public. Some experts expressed concern about consequences of retiring all federal debt held by the public.[72] Most long-term forecasts computed at that time, however, showed large deficits emerging once the baby boomers began to retire. Short-term forecasts projected continuous growth in debt held by government accounts, largely due to the difference between Social Security tax revenues and benefit payments. The combination of falling levels of publicly held debt and rising levels of debt held by government accounts moderated the expected growth of total debt. The moderate growth in total debt those projections had forecast was expected to postpone the need to increase the debt limit until late into the decade, when accumulating debt in government accounts would overtake reductions in debt held by the public.

New budget projections released in early 2002 smashed expectations of large, persistent surpluses, and hopes for reductions in debt held by the public collapsed. The return to large federal deficits accelerated the growth of total debt. Increases in the debt limit would be necessary much sooner than previously expected.

Early in 2003, the FY2003 deficit and the persistent rise in debt held by government accounts drove the federal debt up to the $6,400 billion limit in effect at the time. The Treasury avoided breaching the limit into May. Congress adopted a debt limit increase of $934 billion on May 23, 2003, that provided enough room for the growing federal debt through the fall of 2004. The debt limit increase passed by Congress late in 2004 was expected, at the time, to accommodate the government's debt growth well into 2005, if not into early 2006. In late December 2005, and early in 2006, the Treasury informed Congress that the limit would be reached between mid-February and mid-March 2006. On March 16, 2006, the Senate passed the House-initiated debt limit increase, raising the debt limit to $8,965 billion. The debt limit crisis was resolved when the President signed the debt limit increase on March 20.

Smaller than expected deficits in FY2006 and FY2007 postponed, but did not end the need for a new, higher debt limit. The House passed legislation in May 2007 (H.J.Res. 43) to raise the debt limit. The Senate passed the measure (P.L. 110-91) on September 27, which the President signed on September 29. Turmoil in some financial markets in August 2007, according to some observers, appeared to constrain contention over the debt limit increase.

The 2008 economic slowdown, which reduced federal tax revenues and increased federal outlays, caused federal deficit spending to rise, thus bringing forward the projected date when the federal debt will reach its current limit. The House passed an amended version of the Housing and Economic Recovery Act of 2008 (H.R. 3221) that included a debt limit increase to $10,615 billion on July 23, 2008. The Senate passed the measure on July 26, and the President signed it on July 30, raising the debt limit for the first time in 2008. Subsequently, the Emergency Economic Stabilization Act of 2008 (H.R. 1424), signed into law on October 3 (P.L. 110-343), raised the debt limit for the second time in 2008 to $11,315 billion. The debt limit was raised for the third time in less than a year as a result of passage of the American Recovery and Reinvestment Act of 2009. President Obama signed this measure on February 17, 2009 (P.L. 111-5), which raised the debt limit to $12,104 billion.

The debt limit was again raised in late 2009. H.R. 4314, passed by the House on December 16, 2009, and by the Senate on December 24, raised the debt limit to $12,394 billion when the President signed the measure on December 28. In early 2010, Congress voted for a larger increase in the debt limit, which would put the limit at $14,294 billion, raising the debt ceiling by $1,900 billion. President Obama signed the measure on February 12, 2010. This debt limit, according to projections, will allow the Treasury Department to issue new debt at projected levels until spring 2011.

Amendments offered during consideration of the latest debt limit increase may signal a growing concern with the fiscal sustainability. One amendment, which was not approved, would have established a statutory commission to consider long-term fiscal issues. Another amendment, which was approved, would impose certain PAYGO restrictions.[73] President Obama then created the National Commission on Fiscal Responsibility and Reform (Fiscal Commission), which was charged with identifying "policies to improve the fiscal situation in the medium term and to achieve fiscal sustainability over the long run."[74] A Fiscal Commission report, along with several other budget policy proposals, could provide one framework for changes that might strengthen the federal government's fiscal outlook.[75]

Over the next decade, without major changes in federal policies, persistent and possibly growing deficits, along with the ongoing growth in the debt holdings of government accounts, would increase substantially the amount of federal debt subject to limit. Unless federal policies change, Congress would repeatedly face demands to raise the debt limit to accommodate the growing federal debt in order to provide the government with the means to meet its financial obligations.

## FURTHER READING

Drishnakumar, Anita S., "In Defense of the Debt Limit Statute," *Harvard Journal on Legislation*, vol. 42, 2005, pp. 135-185.

Gordon, John Steele, *Hamilton's Blessing: the Extraordinary Life and Times of Our National Debt*, New York: Penguin, 1998.

Hormats, Robert D., *The Price of Liberty: Paying for America's Wars from the Revolution to the War on Terror*, New York: Times Books, 2007.

Noll, Franklin, "The United States Public Debt, 1861 to 1975," EH.Net Encyclopedia, edited by Robert Whaples, May 26, 2004. Available at http://eh.net/encyclopedia/article/noll.publicdebt.

Wright, Robert E., *One Nation Under Debt: Hamilton, Jefferson, and the History of What We Owe*, New York: McGraw-Hill, 2008.

# APPENDIX. DEBT SUBJECT TO LIMIT BY MONTH SINCE SEPTEMBER 2001

Table A-1 provides data on the dollar amount, in current dollars, of federal debt and the changes in these amounts by month between the end of September 2001 (the end of FY2001) and the end of December 2010. The table shows outstanding monthly balances, subject to the debt limit, of total federal debt, debt held by government accounts, and debt held by the public.

All three measures of debt subject to limit increased over this period. From the end of September 2001 (the end of FY2001) to the end of September 2010 (the most recently completed fiscal year), total federal debt increased by $7,778 billion, debt held in government accounts increased by $2,073 billion, and debt held by the public increased by $5,705 billion. All three measures experienced periodic reductions in some months. Because federal receipts and outlays are spread unevenly over the fiscal year, debt may rise or fall in a given month, even if debt measures follow an overall increasing trend.

## Table A-1. Debt Subject to Limit by Month, September 2001-December 2010 (in millions of current dollars)

| End of Month | Total | Change from Previous Period | Held by Government Accounts | Change from Previous Period | Held by the Public | Change from Previous Period |
|---|---|---|---|---|---|---|
| Sept. 2001 | $5,732,802 | — | $2,436,521 | — | $3,296,281 | — |
| Oct. 2001 | 5,744,523 | $11,721 | 2,451,815 | $15,294 | 3,292,709 | $-3,572 |
| Nov. 2001 | 5,816,823 | 72,300 | 2,469,647 | 17,832 | 3,347,176 | 54,467 |
| Dec. 2001 | 5,871,413 | 54,590 | 2,516,012 | 46,365 | 3,355,401 | 8,225 |
| Jan. 2002 | 5,865,892 | -5,521 | 2,525,755 | 9,743 | 3,340,138 | -15,263 |
| Feb. 2002 | 5,933,154 | 67,262 | 2,528,494 | 2,739 | 3,404,659 | 64,521 |
| Mar. 2002 | 5,935,108 | 1,954 | 2,528,318 | -176 | 3,406,789 | 2,130 |
| Apr. 2002 | 5,914,816 | -20,292 | 2,549,438 | 21,120 | 3,365,378 | -41,411 |
| May 2002 | 5,949,975 | 35,159 | 2,553,350 | 3,912 | 3,396,625 | 31,247 |
| June 2002 | 6,058,313 | 108,338 | 2,630,646 | 77,296 | 3,427,667 | 31,042 |
| July 2002 | 6,092,050 | 33,737 | 2,627,980 | -2,666 | 3,464,070 | 36,403 |
| Aug. 2002 | 6,142,835 | 50,785 | 2,620,946 | -7,034 | 3,521,890 | 57,820 |
| Sept. 2002 | 6,161,431 | 18,596 | 2,644,244 | 23,298 | 3,517,187 | -4,703 |
| Oct. 2002 | 6,231,284 | 69,853 | 2,680,812 | 36,568 | 3,550,472 | 33,285 |
| Nov. 2002 | 6,294,480 | 63,196 | 2,680,788 | -24 | 3,613,692 | 63,220 |

| End of Month | Total | Change from Previous Period | Held by Government Accounts | Change from Previous Period | Held by the Public | Change from Previous Period |
|---|---|---|---|---|---|---|
| Dec. 2002 | 6,359,412 | 64,932 | 2,745,787 | 64,999 | 3,613,625 | -67 |
| Jan. 2003 | 6,355,812 | -3,600 | 2,753,301 | 7,514 | 3,602,511 | -11,114 |
| Feb. 2003 | 6,399,975 | 44,163 | 2,750,471 | -2,830 | 3,649,504 | 46,993 |
| Mar. 2003 | 6,399,975 | 0 | 2,722,812 | -27,659 | 3,677,163 | 27,659 |
| Apr. 2003 | 6,399,975 | 0 | 2,731,042 | 8,230 | 3,668,933 | -8,230 |
| May 2003 | 6,498,658 | 98,683 | 2,755,895 | 24,853 | 3,742,763 | 73,830 |
| June 2003 | 6,625,519 | 126,861 | 2,842,361 | 86,466 | 3,783,158 | 40,395 |
| July 2003 | 6,704,814 | 79,295 | 2,835,566 | -6,795 | 3,869,247 | 86,089 |
| Aug. 2003 | 6,743,775 | 38,961 | 2,829,387 | -6,179 | 3,914,388 | 45,141 |
| Sept. 2003 | 6,737,553 | -6,222 | 2,846,730 | 17,343 | 3,890,823 | -23,565 |
| Oct. 2003 | 6,826,668 | 89,115 | 2,869,493 | 22,763 | 3,957,175 | 66,352 |
| Nov. 2003 | 6,879,626 | 52,958 | 2,879,117 | 9,624 | 4,000,509 | 43,334 |
| Dec. 2003 | 6,952,893 | 73,267 | 2,940,736 | 61,619 | 4,012,157 | 11,648 |
| Jan. 2004 | 6,966,851 | 13,958 | 2,951,219 | 10,483 | 4,015,633 | 3,476 |
| Feb. 2004 | 7,049,163 | 82,312 | 2,953,123 | 1,904 | 4,096,040 | 80,407 |
| Mar. 2004 | 7,088,648 | 39,485 | 2,941,195 | -11,928 | 4,147,453 | 51,413 |
| Apr. 2004 | 7,089,700 | 1,052 | 2,960,151 | 18,956 | 4,129,549 | -17,904 |
| May 2004 | 7,151,523 | 61,823 | 2,973,869 | 13,718 | 4,177,653 | 48,104 |

## Table A-1. (Continued).

| End of Month | Total | Change from Previous Period | Held by Government Accounts | Change from Previous Period | Held by the Public | Change from Previous Period |
|---|---|---|---|---|---|---|
| June 2004 | 7,229,320 | 77,797 | 3,039,987 | 66,118 | 4,189,334 | 11,681 |
| July 2004 | 7,271,328 | 42,008 | 3,033,396 | -6,591 | 4,237,933 | 48,599 |
| Aug. 2004 | 7,305,531 | 34,203 | 3,037,149 | 3,753 | 4,268,382 | 30,449 |
| Sept. 2004 | 7,333,350 | 27,819 | 3,056,590 | 19,441 | 4,276,760 | 8,378 |
| Oct. 2004 | 7,383,975 | 50,625 | 3,096,207 | 39,617 | 4,287,768 | 11,008 |
| Nov. 2004 | 7,464,740 | 80,765 | 3,087,834 | -8,373 | 4,376,906 | 89,138 |
| Dec. 2004 | 7,535,644 | 70,904 | 3,158,531 | 70,697 | 4,377,114 | 208 |
| Jan. 2005 | 7,567,702 | 32,058 | 3,171,089 | 12,558 | 4,396,615 | 19,501 |
| Feb. 2005 | 7,652,726 | 85,024 | 3,176,406 | 5,317 | 4,476,320 | 79,705 |
| Mar. 2005 | 7,715,503 | 62,777 | 3,175,460 | -946 | 4,540,042 | 63,722 |
| Apr. 2005 | 7,704,041 | -11,462 | 3,185,364 | 9,904 | 4,518,677 | -21,365 |
| May 2005 | 7,717,574 | 13,533 | 3,207,232 | 21,868 | 4,510,342 | -8,335 |
| June 2005 | 7,778,128 | 60,554 | 3,280,914 | 73,682 | 4,497,214 | -13,128 |
| July 2005 | 7,829,029 | 50,901 | 3,278,725 | -2,189 | 4,550,304 | 53,090 |
| Aug. 2005 | 7,868,395 | 39,366 | 3,284,696 | 5,971 | 4,583,699 | 33,395 |
| Sept. 2005 | 7,871,040 | 2,645 | 3,300,969 | 16,273 | 4,570,071 | -13,628 |

| End of Month | Total | Change from Previous Period | Held by Government Accounts | Change from Previous Period | Held by the Public | Change from Previous Period |
|---|---|---|---|---|---|---|
| Oct. 2005 | 7,964,782 | 93,742 | 3,345,589 | 44,620 | 4,619,193 | 49,122 |
| Nov. 2005 | 8,028,918 | 64,136 | 3,351,093 | 5,504 | 4,677,826 | 58,633 |
| Dec. 2005 | 8,107,019 | 78,101 | 3,424,304 | 73,211 | 4,682,715 | 4,889 |
| Jan. 2006 | 8,132,290 | 25,271 | 3,442,543 | 18,239 | 4,689,747 | 7,032 |
| Feb. 2006 | 8,183,975 | 51,685 | 3,457,409 | 14,866 | 4,726,567 | 36,820 |
| Mar. 2006 | 8,281,451 | 97,476 | 3,443,602 | -13,807 | 4,837,849 | 111,282 |
| Apr. 2006 | 8,262,718 | -18,733 | 3,479,623 | 36,021 | 4,783,095 | -54,754 |
| May 2006 | 8,263,812 | 1,094 | 3,492,648 | 13,025 | 4,771,165 | -11,930 |
| June 2006 | 8,330,646 | 66,834 | 3,566,186 | 73,538 | 4,764,460 | -6,705 |
| July 2006 | 8,352,614 | 21,968 | 3,569,550 | 3,364 | 4,783,064 | 18,604 |
| Aug. 2006 | 8,423,321 | 70,707 | 3,576,166 | 6,616 | 4,847,155 | 64,091 |
| Sept. 2006 | 8,420,278 | -3,043 | 3,622,378 | 46,212 | 4,828,972 | -18,183 |
| Oct. 2006 | 8,498,016 | 77,738 | 3,650,241 | 27,863 | 4,847,775 | 18,803 |
| Nov. 2006 | 8,545,715 | 47,699 | 3,649,736 | -505 | 4,895,979 | 48,204 |
| Dec. 2006 | 8,592,513 | 46,798 | 3,724,450 | 74,714 | 4,868,063 | -27,916 |
| Jan. 2007 | 8,619,499 | 26,986 | 3,737,894 | 13,444 | 4,881,605 | 13,542 |
| Feb. 2007 | 8,690,921 | 71,422 | 3,744,299 | 6,405 | 4,946,622 | 65,017 |
| Mar. 2007 | 8,760,735 | 69,814 | 3,740,127 | -4,172 | 5,020,608 | 73,986 |

## Table A-1. (Continued).

| End of Month | Total | Change from Previous Period | Held by Government Accounts | Change from Previous Period | Held by the Public | Change from Previous Period |
|---|---|---|---|---|---|---|
| Apr. 2007 | 8,753,070 | -7,665 | 3,778,255 | 38,128 | 4,974,815 | -45,793 |
| May 2007 | 8,740,892 | -12,178 | 3,792,201 | 13,946 | 4,948,691 | -26,124 |
| June 2007 | 8,779,168 | 38,276 | 3,867,819 | 75,618 | 4,911,348 | -37,343 |
| July 2007 | 8,845,417 | 66,249 | 3,873,239 | 5,420 | 4,972,178 | 60,830 |
| Aug. 2007 | 8,918,493 | 73,076 | 3,854,115 | -19,124 | 5,064,377 | 92,199 |
| Sept. 2007 | 8,921,343 | 2,850 | 3,903,710 | 49,595 | 5,017,633 | -46,744 |
| Oct. 2007 | 8,994,639 | 73,296 | 3,958,357 | 54,647 | 5,036,281 | 18,648 |
| Nov. 2007 | 9,065,827 | 71,188 | 3,950,468 | -7,889 | 5,115,358 | 79,077 |
| Dec. 2007 | 9,144,715 | 78,888 | 4,038,566 | 88,098 | 5,106,149 | -9,209 |
| Jan. 2008 | 9,155,842 | 11,127 | 4,053,199 | 14,633 | 5,102,644 | -3,505 |
| Feb. 2008 | 9,275,683 | 119,841 | 4,045,007 | -8,192 | 5,230,676 | 128,032 |
| Mar. 2008 | 9,358,135 | 82,452 | 4,051,685 | 6,678 | 5,306,450 | 75,774 |
| Apr. 2008 | 9,298,567 | -59,568 | 4,080,887 | 29,202 | 5,217,680 | -88,770 |
| May 2008 | 9,324,137 | 25,570 | 4,071,992 | -8,895 | 5,252,144 | 34,464 |
| June 2008 | 9,427,901 | 167,869 | 4,169,509 | 134,950 | 5,258,392 | 32,920 |
| July 2008 | 9,520,220 | 92,319 | 4,144,377 | -25,132 | 5,375,843 | 117,451 |

| | | | | | | |
|---|---|---|---|---|---|---|
| Aug. 2008 | 9,580,508 | 60,288 | 4,129,413 | -14,964 | 5,451,095 | 75,252 |
| Sept. 2008 | 9,959,850 | 379,342 | 4,179,574 | 50,161 | 5,780,276 | 329,181 |
| Oct. 2008 | 10,504,702 | 544,852 | 4,231,878 | 52,304 | 6,272,824 | 492,548 |
| Nov. 2008 | 10,595,725 | 91,023 | 4,228,270 | -3,608 | 6,367,454 | 94,630 |
| Dec. 2008 | 10,640,274 | 44,549 | 4,298,482 | 70,212 | 6,341,792 | -25,662 |
| Jan. 2009 | 10,569,310 | -70,964 | 4,278,424 | -20,058 | 6,290,886 | -50,906 |
| Feb. 2009 | 10,814,630 | 245,320 | 4,261,734 | -16,690 | 6,552,896 | 262,010 |
| Mar. 2009 | 11,066,217 | 251,587 | 4,258,272 | -3,462 | 6,807,946 | 255,050 |
| Apr. 2009 | 11,178,827 | 112,610 | 4,273,005 | 14,733 | 6,905,822 | 97,876 |
| May 2009 | 11,260,445 | 81,618 | 4,265,719 | -7,286 | 6,994,725 | 88,903 |
| June 2009 | 11,487,470 | 227,025 | 4,336,673 | 70,954 | 7,150,797 | 156,072 |
| July 2009 | 11,611,178 | 123,708 | 4,299,673 | -37,000 | 7,311,505 | 160,708 |
| Aug. 2009 | 11,755,205 | 144,027 | 4,294,923 | -4,750 | 7,460,282 | 148,777 |
| Sept. 2009 | 11,853,434 | 98,229 | 4,325,124 | 30,201 | 7,528,311 | 68,029 |
| Oct. 2009 | 11,836,629 | -16,805 | 4,372,308 | 47,184 | 7,464,321 | -63,990 |
| Nov. 2009 | 12,057,363 | 220,734 | 4,367,935 | -4,373 | 7,689,428 | 225,107 |
| Dec. 2009 | 12,254,506 | 197,143 | 4,466,279 | 98,344 | 7,788,227 | 98,799 |
| Jan. 2010 | 12,222,507 | -31,999 | 4,485,502 | 19,223 | 7,737,005 | -51,222 |
| Feb. 2010 | 12,383,717 | 161,210 | 4,469,373 | -16,129 | 7,914,344 | 177,339 |
| Mar. 2010 | 12,716,511 | 332,794 | 4,448,645 | -20,728 | 8,267,866 | 353,522 |

**Table A-1. (Continued).**

| End of Month | Total | Change from Previous Period | Held by Government Accounts | Change from Previous Period | Held by the Public | Change from Previous Period |
|---|---|---|---|---|---|---|
| Apr. 2010 | 12,892,729 | 176,218 | 4,480,458 | 31,813 | 8,412,271 | 144,405 |
| May 2010 | 12,992,539 | 99,810 | 4,498,120 | 17,662 | 8,494,419 | 82,148 |
| June 2010 | 13,149,560 | 157,021 | 4,537,716 | 39,596 | 8,611,844 | 117,425 |
| July 2010 | 13,185,208 | 35,648 | 4,504,601 | -33,115 | 8,680,607 | 68,763 |
| Aug. 2010 | 13,398,794 | 213,586 | 4,493,418 | -11,183 | 8,905,376 | 224,769 |
| Sept. 2010 | 13,510,840 | 112,046 | 4,509,632 | 16,214 | 9,001,208 | 95,832 |
| Oct. 2010 | 13,617,337 | 106,497 | 4,568,895 | 59,263 | 9,048,442 | 47,234 |
| Nov. 2010 | 13,809,121 | 191,784 | 4,555,396 | -13,499 | 9,253,725 | 205,283 |
| Dec. 2010 | 13,972,513 | 163,392 | 4,603,888 | 48,492 | 9,368,625 | 114,900 |

Source: U.S. Treasury, Bureau of the Public Debt, *Monthly Statement of the Public Debt*, Sept. 2001-Nov. 2010, available at http://www.treasurydirect.gov/govt/reports/pd/mspd/mspd.htm; CRS calculations. Dec. 2010 data computed from Daily Treasury Statement.

## End Notes

[1] Approximately 0.5% of total debt is excluded from debt limit coverage. The Treasury defines "Total Public Debt Subject to Limit" as "the Total Public Debt Outstanding less Unamortized Discount on Treasury Bills and Zero-Coupon Treasury Bonds, old debt issued prior to 1917, and old currency called United States Notes, as well as Debt held by the Federal Financing Bank and Guaranteed Debt." For details, see http://www.treasury direct.gov. The debt limit is codified as 31 USC 3101.

[2] Although there are hundreds of trust funds, the overwhelming majority are very small. The 12 largest trust funds hold 98.8% of the federal debt held in government accounts.

[3] Other means of financing—including cash balance changes, seigniorage, and capitalization of financing accounts used to fund federal credit programs—have relatively little effect on the changes in debt held by the public.

[4] In future years, when some trust funds are projected to pay out more than they take in, funds that the Treasury would use to redeem those intergovernmental debts must be obtained via higher taxes or lower government spending.

[5] Trust fund surpluses by law must be invested in special federal government securities.

[6] Daily data on federal debt can be obtained at the Treasury Department's Bureau of the Public Debt website: http://www.treasurydirect.gov/NP/BPDLogin?application=np. Data on debt subject to limit are provided in the *Daily Treasury Statement*, available at http://fms. treas.gov/dts/index.html.

[7] U.S. Treasury, "Treasury Announces Marketable Borrowing Estimates," press release TG-1038, January 31, 2011, available at http://www.treasury.gov/press-center/press-releases/Pages/ tg1038.aspx.

[8] U.S. Congressional Budget Office, *The Budget and Economic Outlook*, January 26, 2011, available at http://www.cbo.gov/doc.cfm?index=12039.

[9] U.S. Treasury, "Treasury Assistant Secretary for Financial Markets Mary Miller February 2011 Quarterly Refunding Statement," press release TG-1045, February 2, 2011, available at http://www.treasury.gov/press-center/press-releases/ Pages/tg1045.aspx.

[10] Wrightson ICAP, *The Money Market Observer*, December 13, 2010.

[11] Paul M. Krawzak, "Showdown Ahead on Debt Limit as Geithner Urges Action," *CQ Today Online News*, January 6, 2011; Secretary of the U.S. Treasury Timothy Geithner, letter to Majority Leader Harry Reid, dated January 6, 2011.

[12] For details, see the CRS congressional distribution memorandum *Reaching the Debt Limit*, December 28, 2010, coordinated by Mindy R. Levit. This memorandum is available upon request by congressional offices.

[13] 31 U.S.C. §3902.

[14] 26 U.S.C. §6611.

[15] For details, see archived CRS Report 95-1109, *Authority to Tap Trust Funds and Establish Payment Priorities if the Debt Limit is not Increased*, by Thomas J. Nicola and Morton Rosenberg. Available upon request from authors. 5 U.S.C. Sec. 8348(b) defines a debt issuance suspension period as "any period for which the Secretary of the Treasury determines for purposes of this subsection that the issuance of obligations of the United States may not be made without exceeding the public debt limit." After a debt issuance suspension period ends, the Treasury Secretary must report to Congress as soon as possible regarding fund balances and any extraordinary actions taken. For details, see 5 USC Sec. 8348(j,k).

[16] U.S. General Accounting Office (GAO), *Analysis of Actions Taken during the 2003 Debt Issuance Suspension Period,* GAO-04-526, May 2004, available at http://www.gao.gov/new.items/d04526.pdf.

[17] For a vigorous assertion of the utility of the debt ceiling, see Anita S. Drishnakumar, "In Defense of the Debt Limit Statute," *Harvard Journal on Legislation*, vol. 42, 2005, pp. 135-185.

[18] Marshall A. Robinson, *The National Debt Ceiling: An Experiment in Fiscal Policy*, Washington, DC: The Brookings Institution, 1959, p. 5.

[19] Bruce Bartlett, "Why Congress Must Now Abolish its Debt Limit," *Financial Times*, October 22, 2009, p. 11.

[20] P.L. 65-43, 40 Stat. 288, enacted September 24, 1917. Currently codified as amended as 31 U.S.C. § 3101.

[21] H. J. Cooke and M. Katzen, "The Public Debt Limit," *Journal of Finance*, vol. 9, no. 3 (September 1954), pp. 298-303.

[22] Robert D. Hormats, *The Price of Liberty,* (New York: Henry Holt, 2007), ch. 4.

[23] Treasury certificates of indebtedness were short-term, interest-bearing securities. Treasury bills are securities with a maturity of a year or less. Treasury notes are interest-bearing securities that generally have maturities of two to five years. Treasury bonds are interest-bearing securities that generally have maturities of 10 or more years.

[24] Marshall A. Robinson, *The National Debt Ceiling: An Experiment in Fiscal Policy*, (Washington, DC: The Brookings Institution, 1959), pp.1-6.

[25] The War Revenue Act, formally "An Act to Provide Ways and Means to Meet War Expenditures and for Other Purposes," was enacted June 13, 1898. Much of the legislative text of the Act's public borrowing sections (§32, 33) were drawn from the Acts of June 30, 1864, ch. 172, §1 (13 Stats. 218) and of March 3, 1865, ch. 77 (13 Stats. 469).

[26] Some opponents raised concerns that granting the Treasury Secretary authority to issue debt could affect monetary policies, which might tighten credit conditions. Such concerns became less relevant after the establishment of the Federal Reserve System in 1913. See House debate, *Congressional Record*, vol. 31, part 6 (June 9, 1898), pp. 5713-5728; and Senate debate on June 10, 1898, pp. 5734-5749.

[27] P.L. 76-201. Some authors claimed the aggregate limit was first created in Public Debt Act of 1941 (P.L. 77-7). The 1939 Senate floor debate, however, makes clear that Congress intended to lift categorical debt restrictions. See Senate debate, *Congressional Record*, vol. 84, part 6 (June 1, 1939), pp. 6480, 6497-6501.

[28] This limit did not apply to certain previous public debt issues that constituted a minor portion of the federal debt.

[29] U.S. Bureau of the Census, *Historical Statistics of the United States: Colonial Times to 1970*, H. Doc. 93-78 (Washington: GPO, 1975), Series Y 493-504.

[30] Public Debt Acts of 1941 (P.L. 77-7), 1942 (P.L. 77-510), 1943 (78-34), 1944 (P.L. 78-333), and 1945 (P.L. 79-48).

[31] U.S. Office of Management and Budget, *FY2010 Budget of the U.S. Government: Historical Tables*, Table 7-3.

[32] Until 2001, Treasury publications did not divide debt subject to limit by that held by the public and that held by government accounts. Table 1 uses CRS calculations that approximate levels of debt subject to limit held in these two categories for fiscal years prior to 2001.

[33] The data show components of debt compared to the size of the economy. This avoids possible distortions resulting from changing price levels over time and includes changes in per capita

incomes. This percentage increases when debt grows faster than GDP and falls when it grows more slowly than GDP.

[34] Federal on-budget receipts and outlays nearly matched in FY1999, and the on-budget surplus in FY2000 was 0.9% of GDP. Prior to FY1999, the federal government last had an on-budget surplus in FY1960. Social Security receipts in excess of benefits make up most of the off-budget surplus, which has been positive since FY1985.

[35] U.S. Congress, Congressional Budget Office, An Analysis of the President's Budgetary Proposals for Fiscal Year 2009, March 2008, available at http://www.cbo.gov/ftpdocs/89xx/doc8990/03-19-AnalPresBudget.pdf.

[36] The debt limit was raised from $5,500 billion to $5,950 billion on August 5, 1997, as part of the Balanced Budget Act of 1997 (P.L. 105-33, 111 Stat. 251).

[37] For a comprehensive discussion of the Treasury's previous uses of its short-term ability to avoid breaching the debt limit, see U.S. General Accounting Office, *Debt Ceiling: Analysis of Actions During the 1995-1996 Crisis*, GAO/AIMD-96-130, August 1996.

[38] U.S. Department of the Treasury, Treasury News, *Treasury Statement on the Debt Ceiling*, May 14, 2002.

[39] For additional details, see U.S. General Accounting Office, *Debt Ceiling: Analysis of Actions During the 2002 Debt Issuance Suspension Period*, GAO-03-134, December 2002.

[40] Kenneth Dam, Deputy Secretary of the Treasury, letter to Speaker of the House, Dennis Hastert, December 24, 2002, available at http://www.treas.gov/press/releases/po3718.htm.

[41] The Treasury reduced the amount of debt held by selected federal accounts while it sold an equal (or smaller) amount of debt to the public. This raised cash needed to pay for ongoing obligations and kept the debt below the limit.

[42] The House Budget Committee has some discretion in setting the debt limit level in the House Joint resolution generated by the Gephardt rule. See CRS Report 98-453, *Debt-Limit Legislation in the Congressional Budget Process*, by Bill Heniff Jr. and CRS Report RL31913, *Developing Debt-Limit Legislation: The House's "Gephardt Rule"*, by Bill Heniff Jr..

[43] U.S. Congress, Congressional Budget Office, *The Budget and Economic Outlook: Fiscal Years 2005 to 2014*, January 2004.

[44] Alan Fram, "Congress May Duck Debt Limit Raise," *Oakland Tribune*, June 5, 2004.

[45] John W. Snow, Secretary of the U.S. Treasury, letter to Senate Majority Leader Bill Frist, October 14, 2004, available at http://www.treas.gov/press/releases/reports/frist.pdf.

[46] John W. Snow, Secretary of the Treasury, letter to Senator Max Baucus, December 29, 2005, available at http://www.ombwatch.org/files/budget/pdf/snow_debtlimit_2006.pdf.

[47] The end of a recession is said to occur when an economy has stopped shrinking, not when it has recovered. See National Bureau of Economic Research Business Cycle Dating Committee, press release, September 20, 2010, available at http://www.nber.org/cycles

[48] U.S. Congress, Congressional Budget Office, *An Analysis of the President's Budgetary Proposals for Fiscal Year 2009*, Table 1.1, March 2008, available at http://www.cbo.gov/ftpdocs/89xx/doc8990/03-19-AnalPresBudget.pdf.

[48] U.S. Congress, Congressional Budget Office, *The Budget and Economic Outlook: An Update*, Table 1-1, August 2009, available at http://www.cbo.gov/doc.cfm?index=10521.

[49] Goldman Sachs U.S. Research, "US Daily: The Fiscal 2008 Deficit—Likely to Top $500 Billion," March 25, 2008.

[50] U.S. Congress, House Committee on the Budget, *Report to Accompany H. Con. Res. 312*, 110th Cong., 2nd sess., H.Rept. 110-543, March 2008, p. 99; U.S. Congress, Senate Committee on the Budget, *Report to Accompany S. Res. 70*, S.Prt. 110-039, March 2008.

[51] U.S. Congress, Congressional Budget Office, *Cost Estimate for H.R. 3221 "Housing and Economic Recovery Act of 2008" As passed by the Senate on July 11, 2008, with an amendment transmitted to CBO on July 22, 2008*, July 24, 2008, available at http://www.cbo.gov/ftpdocs/95xx/doc9597/hr3221.pdf.

[52] For additional information see CRS Report RS22956, *The Cost of Government Financial Interventions, Past and Present*, by Baird Webel, Marc Labonte, and N. Eric Weiss.

[53] U.S. Department of Treasury, "Fact Sheet: Proposed Treasury Authority to Purchase Troubled Assets," Press release hp-1150, Sept. 20, 2008, available at http://www.treas.gov/press/releases/hp1150.htm.

[54] U.S. Congress, House Financial Services Committee, Emergency Economic Stabilization Act of 2008 (Amendment to the Senate Amendment to H.R. 3997), available at http://www.house.gov/apps/list/press/financialsvcs_dem/amend_001_xml.pdf. For text of debt limit provision, see *Congressional Record*, (Sept. 29, 2008), p. H10355.

[55] U.S. Congress, Senate Banking, Housing, and Urban Affairs Committee, Emergency Economic Stabilization Act of 2008 (In the Nature of a Substitute to H.R. 1424), available at http://banking latestversionAYO08C32_xml.pdf.

[56] *CQ Weekly*, "Fall 2009 Outlook: Debt Limit Increase," September 7, 2009, p. 1966.

[57] U.S. Treasury, "November 2009 Quarterly Refunding Statement," press release tg346, November 4, 2009, http://www.ustreas.gov/press/releases/tg346.htm; David Clarke and CQ Staff, "Treasury Gives Congress More Breathing Room on Debt Limit," *CQ Today Online News*, November 4, 2009.

[58] For details, see Joseph Haubrich and John Lindner, "The Supplemental Financing Program," *Economic Trends,* Federal Reserve of Chicago, September 28, 2009, available at http://www.clevelandfed.org/research/trends/2009/1009/ 03monpol.cfm.

[59] *The Money Market Observer: Wrightson ICAP's Weekly Newsletter*, December 7, 2009.

[60] *The Money Market Observer: Wrightson ICAP's Weekly Newsletter*, November 30, 2009.

[61] Paul Kane, "House Democrats Discard Larger Debt Limit," *Washington Post*, December 15, 2009, p. A4.

[62] *CQ Today Midday Update*, "Senate Sends Debt Ceiling Increase to House," January 28, 2010.

[63] S.Amdt. 3305. A second amendment (S.Amdt. 3300), approved on a 97-0 vote, provides certain protections to the Social Security program. Other amendments were not approved.

[64] Jonathan Weisman and John D. McKinnon, "White House Weighs New Panel to Tackle Deficit: Bipartisan Commission Considered As Administration Seeks to Show Resolve on a Problem that Dogs Its Broader Agenda," *Wall Street Journal*, November 26, 2009, p. A10.

[65] Executive Order 13531, "National Commission on Fiscal Responsibility and Reform," February 18, 2010; 75 FR 7927, February 23, 2010.

[66] National Commission on Fiscal Responsibility and Reform, *The Moment of Truth*, report, December 1, 2010, available at http://www.fiscalcommission.gov/sites/ fiscalcommission.gov/files/documents/ TheMomentofTruth12_1_2010.pdf.

[67] U.S. Office of Management and Budget, "H.J.Res. 45—Increasing the Statutory Limit on the Public Debt," Statement Of Administration Policy, January 20, 2010, available at http://www.whitehouse.gov/omb/assets saphjr45s_20100120.pdf.

[68] For a discussion of earlier debt limit increases, see CRS Report 98-805 E, *Public Debt Limit Legislation: A Brief History and Controversies In the 1980s and 1990s*, by Philip D. Winters, which is available from the authors upon request.

[69] U.S. Congressional Budget Office, *The Budget and Economic Outlook: An Update*, August 19, 2010, p. 1, available at http://www.cbo.gov/doc.cfm?index=11705.

[70] The ability to run fiscal deficits gives the federal government useful flexibility in managing its finances, although large deficits may harm economic performance. See CRS Report RL33657, *Running Deficits: Positives and Pitfalls*, by D. Andrew Austin.

[71] *Report of the National Commission on Social Security Reform*, January 1983, available at http://www.ssa.gov/history/reports/gspan.html.

[72] Testimony of Federal Reserve Chairman Alan Greenspan, in U.S. Congress, Senate Committee on the Budget, *Outlook for the Federal Budget and Implications for Fiscal Policy*, hearings, 107th Cong., 1st sess., January 25, 2001, available at http://www.federalreserve.gov/ boarddocs/testimony/2001/20010125/default.htm.

[73] For a discussion of PAYGO in the past, see CRS Report R41005, *The Statutory PAYGO Process for Budget Enforcement: 1991-2002*, by Robert Keith.

[74] Executive Order 13531, "National Commission on Fiscal Responsibility and Reform," February 18, 2010; 75 FR 7927, February 23, 2010.

[75] National Commission on Fiscal Responsibility and Reform, *The Moment of Truth*, report, December 1, 2010, available at http://www.fiscalcommission.gov/ sites/ fiscalcommission. gov/files/documents/ TheMomentofTruth12_1_2010.pdf.

In: Debt Limit Management... ISBN: 978-1-61324-418-0
Editors: J. D. Antonellis, N. P. Barone 

*Chapter 3*

# DEBT LIMIT: DELAYS CREATE DEBT MANAGEMENT CHALLENGES AND INCREASE UNCERTAINTY IN THE TREASURY MARKET*

***United States Government Accountability Office***

## WHY GAO DID THIS STUDY

GAO has prepared this report to assist Congress in identifying and addressing debt management challenges. Since 1995, the statutory debt limit has been increased 12 times to its current level of $14.294 trillion. The Department of the Treasury (Treasury) recently notified Congress that the current debt limit could be reached as early as April 5, 2011, and the Congressional Budget Office (CBO) projects that under current law debt subject to the limit will exceed $25 trillion in 2021.

This report (1) describes the actions that Treasury traditionally takes to manage debt near the limit, (2) analyzes the effects that approaching the debt limit has had on the market for Treasury securities, and (3) describes alternative mechanisms that would permit consideration of the link between policy decisions and the effect on debt when or before decisions are made.

---

* This is an edited, reformatted and augmented version of the United States Government Accountability Office's publication, dated February 2011.

GAO analyzed Treasury and market data; interviewed Treasury officials, budget and legislative experts, and market participants; and reviewed practices in selected countries.

## What GAO Recommends

To avoid potential disruptions to Treasury markets and help inform fiscal policy decisions in a timely way, Congress should consider ways to better link decisions about the debt limit with decisions about spending and revenue.

Treasury provided technical comments on a draft of this report, which GAO incorporated as appropriate.

## What GAO Found

The debt limit does not control or limit the ability of the federal government to run deficits or incur obligations. Rather, it is a limit on the ability to pay obligations already incurred.

While debates surrounding the debt limit may raise awareness about the federal government's current debt trajectory and may also provide Congress with an opportunity to debate the fiscal policy decisions driving that trajectory, the ability to have an immediate effect on debt levels is limited. This is because the debt reflects previously enacted tax and spending policies.

Delays in raising the debt limit create debt and cash management challenges for the Treasury, and these challenges have been exacerbated in recent years by a large growth in debt. In the past, Treasury has often used extraordinary actions, such as suspending investments or temporarily disinvesting securities held in federal employee retirement funds, to remain under the statutory limit. However, the extraordinary actions available to the Treasury have not kept pace with the growth in borrowing needs. For example, unlike the past, the amount potentially provided by the extraordinary actions for 1 month in fiscal year 2010 was less than the monthly increase in debt subject to the limit for most months of the year. As a result, once debt reaches the limit, Congress will likely have less time than in prior years to debate raising the debt limit before there are disruptions to government programs and services. This trend is likely to continue given the long-term fiscal outlook.

Failure to raise the debt limit in a timely manner could have serious negative consequences for the Treasury market and increase borrowing costs. Also, some of the actions that Treasury has taken to manage the amount of debt near the limit add uncertainty to the Treasury market. In the past, Treasury has postponed auctions and dramatically reduced the amount of bills outstanding, which compromised the regularity of auctions and the certainty of supply on which Treasury relies to achieve the lowest borrowing cost over time. GAO's analysis suggests that borrowing costs modestly increased during debt limit debates in 2002, 2003, and most recently in 2010.

In addition, managing debt near the debt limit diverts Treasury's limited resources away from other cash and debt management issues at a time when Treasury already faces challenges in lengthening the average maturity of its debt portfolio.

Observers and participants suggested improving the link between the spending and revenue decisions that drive debt and changes in the debt limit. Better alignment could be possible if decisions about the debt level occur in conjunction with spending and revenue decisions as opposed to the after-the-fact approach now used. This practice, which is similar to practices used in some other countries, might facilitate efforts to change the fiscal path by highlighting the implications of tax and spending decisions on changes in debt.

## ABBREVIATIONS

| | |
|---|---|
| BPD | Bureau of the Public Debt |
| CBO | Congressional Budget Office |
| CDS | credit default swap |
| CPFF | Commercial Paper Funding Facility |
| CM bill | cash management bill |
| CSRDF | Civil Service Retirement and Disability Fund |
| DISP | debt issuance suspension period |
| ESF | Exchange Stabilization Fund |
| FFB | Federal Financing Bank |
| G-Fund | Government Securities Investment Fund of the Federal Employees' Retirement System |
| GDP | gross domestic product |
| IMF | International Monetary Fund |
| LIBOR | London interbank offer rate |
| Moody's | Moody's Investors Service |

| | |
|---|---|
| ODM | Office of Debt Management |
| OECD | Organisation for Economic Co-operation and Development |
| OFP | Office of Fiscal Projections |
| Recovery Act | American Recovery and Reinvestment Act of 2009 |
| Secretary | Secretary of the Treasury |
| SFP | Supplementary Financing Program |
| SLGS | State and Local Government Series |
| TARP | Troubled Asset Relief Program |
| TIPS | Treasury Inflation-Protected Securities |
| Treasury | Department of the Treasury |
| VIX | Chicago Board Options Exchange's Volatility Index |

February 22, 2011

Report to the Congress

Congress and the President have enacted laws to establish a limit on the amount of federal debt that can be outstanding at one time. The debt limit does not restrict Congress' ability to enact spending and revenue legislation that affect the level of debt or otherwise constrain fiscal policy; it restricts the Department of the Treasury's (Treasury) authority to borrow to finance the decisions enacted by the Congress and the President. As a result, as the government nears the debt limit, Treasury often must deviate from its normal cash and debt management operations and take a number of extraordinary actions such as temporarily disinvesting securities held as part of federal employees' retirement plans to meet the government's obligations as they come due without exceeding the debt limit. Once the extraordinary actions are exhausted, Treasury is not authorized to issue new debt and could be forced to delay payments for government services or operations until funding is available and could eventually be forced to default on legal debt obligations.

Since 1995, the statutory debt limit has been increased 12 times to its current level of $14.294 trillion. Treasury recently notified Congress that the current debt limit could be reached as early as April 5, 2011, and the Congressional Budget Office (CBO) projects that, if current laws remain in place, debt subject to the limit will exceed $25 trillion in 2021. Meanwhile, GAO's long-term simulations show that absent policy changes, federal debt will increase continually over the next several decades. The medium- and long-term outlook for the federal budget makes an understanding of the operations and implications of the debt limit important.

GAO has prepared this report under the Comptroller General's authority to conduct evaluations on his own initiative as part of a continuing effort to assist Congress in identifying and addressing debt management challenges. This report examines the challenges associated with managing cash and debt near the limit. Specifically, the objectives of this report are to (1) describe the actions that Treasury has taken to manage debt near the limit and challenges that arise, (2) analyze the effects that approaching the debt limit has on the market for Treasury securities, including Treasury's borrowing costs, and (3) in light of the disconnect between the debt limit and the policy decisions that have an effect on the size of federal debt, describe alternative triggers or mechanisms that would permit consideration of the link between policy decisions and their effect on debt when or before decisions are made.

To answer our first objective, we analyzed publicly available data on Treasury cash and debt transactions from the last 16 years (1995-2010) to identify factors that could create challenges for Treasury in managing debt near or at the limit. We reviewed documents provided by Treasury, interviewed Treasury officials, and obtained estimates of the time and staff involved in planning for when the debt limit will be reached and related operations. We conducted a check for reasonableness of these estimates.

To determine what effect approaching the debt limit had on the Treasury market, we analyzed changes in the size and timing of Treasury auctions when debt was near or at the limit. Our review generally covered the last 16 years—or as many of those years for which data were readily available—in order to include both a particularly disruptive debt limit debate in 1995-1996 that required Treasury to take a number of extraordinary actions and the most recent debt limit increase. We interviewed several market participants and observers, including primary dealers, money market fund managers, and credit rating agencies, to obtain their views on how the debt limit and the actions Treasury takes to manage the amount of debt when it is near the debt limit affect the Treasury market. We analyzed changes in the yields for Treasury securities before, during, and after five of the debt limit debates in the past 10 years, including the most recent in 2009-2010, to determine how proximity to the debt limit affected Treasury's borrowing costs. See appendix II for more details on how we estimated increased borrowing costs including limitations to our analysis.

To identify alternative triggers or other mechanisms, we interviewed budget and legislative experts including former congressional staff; former

CBO, Office of Management and Budget, and Treasury officials; and other congressional observers from a range of policy research organizations. We also reviewed information from select member countries of the Organisation for Economic Co-operation and Development (OECD) and received input from budget or debt office representatives from Canada, Denmark, New Zealand, Sweden, Switzerland, and the United Kingdom about mechanisms used in their countries to manage aggregate levels of debt. We selected these countries based on a review of relevant reports and other information published by the OECD and International Monetary Fund (IMF). While selected countries offer illustrative examples, their experiences are not always applicable to the United States given differences in political systems and economies.

To assess the reliability of the data used in this report, including financial markets data downloaded from Thomson Reuters' proprietary statistical database, Datastream, and IHS Global Insight and publicly available data from Treasury and the Federal Reserve, we examined the data to look for outliers and anomalies and, when possible, compared data from multiple sources for consistency. In general, we chose databases that were commonly used by Treasury and researchers to monitor changes in federal debt and related transactions. On the basis of our assessment we believe the data are sufficiently reliable for the purpose of this review.

We conducted our work from December 2009 to January 2011 in accordance with generally accepted government auditing standards. Those standards require that we plan and perform the audit to obtain sufficient, appropriate evidence to provide a reasonable basis for our findings and conclusions based on our audit objectives. We believe that the evidence obtained provides a reasonable basis for our findings and conclusions based on our audit objectives.

## BACKGROUND

Congress and the President first enacted a statutory limit on federal debt during World War I to eliminate the need for Congress to approve each new debt issuance and provide Treasury with greater discretion over how it finances the government's day-to-day borrowing needs. Federal debt subject to the limit includes both debt held by the public and debt held by government accounts (intragovernmental debt holdings). The majority of debt held by the public consists of marketable Treasury securities, such as bills, notes, bonds, and Treasury Inflation-Protected Securities (TIPS), that are sold through auctions and can be resold by whoever owns them. Treasury also issues a smaller amount of nonmarketable securities, such as savings securities and special securities for state and local governments. Debt held by the public primarily represents the amount the federal government has borrowed to finance cumulative cash deficits. Intragovernmental debt holdings represent balances of Treasury securities held in government accounts such as the Social Security trust funds. It increases when these accounts run a surplus or accrue interest on existing securities.[1] Debt subject to the limit increased from roughly $43 billion in 1940 to more than $13,000 billion (or $13 trillion) in 2010.

In the past, Congress has sought to link decisions about the level of debt to those about the level of federal spending and revenue by integrating changes to the debt limit into the larger budget process. For example, the Congressional Budget Act of 1974 requires that Congress include the levels of debt implied by the spending and revenue levels in the budget resolution for the next 5 years and allows for specific estimates of the increase in debt subject to the limit.[2] Until recently, the House of Representatives had a rule that automatically generated a joint resolution considered to have been passed in the House changing the debt limit by the amount recommended in the budget resolution for the next fiscal year.[3] The Congressional Budget Act as amended also established an alternative procedure for changing the debt limit through reconciliation legislation that is subject to expedited procedures. Despite these rules and procedures, Congress usually votes on the debt limit after fiscal policy decisions affecting federal borrowing have begun to take effect.

Debt limit increases frequently involve protracted debate, regardless of prior votes on the budget resolution or other legislation that increases the need to borrow. This debate often occurs when federal debt is near or at the debt limit. Three pieces of legislation enacted to respond to the financial market crisis and economic downturn are recent exceptions—in each of these the debt limit was increased by roughly the amount the legislation was expected to increase debt. For example, in addition to spending and revenue provisions, the American Recovery and Reinvestment Act of 2009 (Recovery Act) increased the debt limit by $789 billion from $11,315 billion to $12,104 billion.[4] Federal debt at the time of enactment was more than $600 billion below the limit.

Treasury's normal cash management operations involve ensuring that there is enough cash on hand to pay government obligations as they come due. Treasury has two primary sources of funds to finance these obligations: (1)

revenue collections, such as federal tax revenues and other fees the federal government imposes and (2) cash borrowed from the public through auctions of marketable securities. One of Treasury's goals is to finance the government's borrowing needs at the lowest cost over time by, among other things, issuing a wide range of securities in a regular and predictable pattern.[5] Treasury currently issues bills that mature in a year or less, notes with maturities of 2 to 10 years, and bonds with maturities of greater than 10 years. Treasury also issues 5-year, 10- year, and 30-year TIPS, which offer inflation protection to investors who are willing to pay a premium for this protection in the form of lower interest rates.[6] Treasury does not "time the market"—or seek to take advantage of low interest rates—when it issues securities. Instead, Treasury strives to lower its borrowing costs over time by relying on a regular preannounced schedule of auctions.

Treasury holds cash in its operating cash balance in an account at the Federal Reserve and in accounts at depository institutions across the country. Treasury can draw down its operating cash balance as debt approaches the limit, which allows Treasury to temporarily make payments without increasing the amount of debt subject to the limit.

However, cash balances in its account at the Federal Reserve must be kept at a sufficient level to avoid overdrawing this account since the Federal Reserve System cannot legally lend directly to the Treasury.

The issuance of cash management bills (CM bills) provides another way for Treasury to manage more closely the amount of additional debt subject to the limit. CM bills are flexible securities that Treasury issues outside of its regular preannounced auction schedule. Treasury sets the amount and time to maturity to meet its immediate borrowing needs at the time.[7] Issuing CM bills allows Treasury to borrow cash for shorter periods than regular bills to help manage the uncertainty around the timing of increases to the debt limit. However, our past work showed that Treasury paid a premium, in the form of higher yields, for CM bills relative to regular bills.[8]

There are also a number of extraordinary actions currently available to Treasury to avoid exceeding the debt limit. These actions reduce uncertainty over future increases in debt subject to the limit or reduce the amount of debt subject to the limit. Table 1 provides an overview of each one. Two of these actions relate to the Civil Service Retirement and Disability Fund (CSRDF), which is the trust fund for two federal retirement plans that hold nonmarketable securities. To take these actions, Treasury must declare in advance a debt issuance suspension period (DISP)—a period in which

Treasury determines that it cannot issue debt without exceeding the debt limit. Another four actions can be taken without first declaring a DISP.

**Table 1. Extraordinary Actions Taken by Treasury to Manage Debt near the Debt Limit**

| Extraordinary actions that do not require the declaration of a DISP | |
|---|---|
| Suspension of new issuances of State and Local Government Series (SLGS) Securities | SLGS are special securities offered to state and local governments and other issuers of tax-exempt bonds. Suspending new SLGS issuances reduces uncertainty over future increases in debt subject to the limit. Suspending SLGS issuances eliminates a flexible, low-cost option that state and local government issuers have frequently used when refinancing their existing debt before maturity. Suspending new SLGS issuances is generally the first extraordinary action Treasury takes to manage debt near the debt limit. |
| Exchanging Federal Financing Bank (FFB) debt for debt subject to the limit | FFB is a government corporation under the general supervision and direction of the Secretary of the Treasury, which borrows from the Treasury to finance purchases of agency debt and agency guaranteed debt. It can also issue up to $15 billion of its own debt—FFB 9(a) obligations—that is not subject to the debt limit. This debt can be exchanged with other federal debt (e.g., securities held by the CSRDF) to reduce the amount of debt subject to the limit. |
| Suspension of investments to the Government Securities Investment Fund of the Federal Employees' Retirement System (G-Fund)[a] | The G-Fund contains contributions made by federal employees toward their retirement as part of the Thrift Savings Plan program, which are invested in special one-day nonmarketable Treasury securities that are subject to the limit. As debt nears the limit and the Secretary determines that the G-Fund may not be fully invested without exceeding the debt limit, Treasury can suspend investment for the entire amount or a portion of the G-Fund on a daily basis to reduce debt subject to the limit. Treasury is required to restore lost interest on the GFund's uninvested funds after the debt limit has been increased.[b] |

**Table 1. (Continued).**

| | |
|---|---|
| Extraordinary actions that do not require the declaration of a DISP | |
| Suspension of Exchange Stabilization Fund (ESF) Investments | The ESF is used to help provide a stable system of monetary exchange rates. Dollar-denominated assets of the ESF not used for program purposes are generally invested in one-day nonmarketable Treasury securities that are subject to the debt limit. When debt approaches the limit, Treasury can suspend investment for the entire amount or a portion of the ESF's maturing nonmarketable Treasury securities. Treasury is not authorized to restore lost interest to the ESF when the debt limit is increased. |
| Extraordinary actions that require the declaration of a DISP | |
| Suspension of new CSRDF investmentsc | Once debt reaches the debt limit, Treasury is able to suspend investment of new receipts to the CSRDF. To do so, Treasury must send a letter notifying Congress that CSRDF receipts cannot be invested without exceeding the debt limit (i.e., declaring a DISP). Treasury is required to make the CSRDF whole after the DISP has ended. |
| Disinvestment of securities held by CSRDFc | Once debt reaches the debt limit, Treasury is able to disinvest Treasury securities held by theCSRDF. To do so, Treasury must send a letter notifying Congress that it will not be able to issue debt securities without exceeding the debt limit and provide the expected length of the DISP, which Treasury uses to determine the amount of CSRDF investments that can be disinvested. Treasury is required to restore lost interest after the DISP has ended. |

Source: GAO.

[a] Under 5 U.S.C. § 8438(g), to repay lost interest on suspended G-Fund investments, Treasury must declare a separate DISP unrelated to the actions taken involving the CSRDF. The Secretary is required to notify Congress when a G-Fund DISP begins but is not required to determine the length of a G-Fund DISP in advance. For the purposes of this report, we use the term DISP to refer to the authorities that Treasury has related to the CSRDF under 5 U.S.C. § 8348(j) unless otherwise specified.

[b] 5 U.S.C. § 8438(g). [c5] U.S.C. § 8348(j).

Since 1995, the debt limit has been increased 12 times. Prior to 6 of these, Treasury had to take one or more extraordinary actions to avoid exceeding the debt limit. Figure 1 shows when the debt limit was increased and the extraordinary actions that were used.

- Prior to five of the six debt limit increases between 1996 and 2006, Treasury took extraordinary actions, including declaring a DISP.
- During the period immediately preceding the debt limit increase in August 1997, Treasury did not take any extraordinary actions.
- The federal government ran budget surpluses in fiscal years 1998 through 2001. Debt subject to the limit increased by $293 billion during this period, but no increases to the debt limit were required.
- During the period immediately preceding the debt limit increase in September 2007, Treasury suspended the issuance of SLGS but did not take any other extraordinary actions or declare a DISP.
- In 2008 and 2009, three laws that were expected to increase the amount of debt held by the public included corresponding increases in the debt limit at the time of enactment.
- In December 2009 and February 2010, Treasury avoided taking extraordinary actions as debt approached the limit in part by allowing the Treasury securities it issued for the Supplementary Financing Program (SFP)—a temporary program begun in 2008 at the request of the Federal Reserve to drain reserves from the banking system and assist with its emergency liquidity and lending initiatives—to mature without rolling them over.

| | | March 29, 1996 | August 5, 1997 | June 28, 2002 | May 27, 2003 | November 19, 2004 | March 20, 2006 | September 29, 2007 | July 30, 2008 | October 3, 2008 | February 17, 2009 | December 28, 2009 | February 12, 2010 | Total number of times used since 1996 |
|---|---|---|---|---|---|---|---|---|---|---|---|---|---|---|
| Extraordinary actions that do not require the declaration of a DISP | Suspension of new issuances of SLGS | ✓ | | ✓ | ✓ | ✓ | ✓ | ✓ | | | | | | 6 |
| | Exchanging FFB debt for debt subject to the limit[a] | ✓ | | | ✓ | ✓ | | | | | | | | 3 |
| | Suspension of G-Fund investments | ✓ | | ✓ | ✓ | ✓ | ✓ | | | | | | | 5 |
| | Suspension of ESF investments | ✓ | | | ✓ | ✓ | ✓ | | | | | | | 4 |
| Extraordinary actions that require the declaration of a DISP | Suspension of new CSRDF investments | ✓ | | ✓ | ✓ | ✓ | ✓ | | | | | | | 5 |
| | Disinvestment of securities held by CSRDF | ✓ | | ✓ | ✓ | ✓ | ✓ | | | | | | | 5 |

Figure 1. Extraordinary Actions Taken by Treasury Prior to Debt Limit Increases, 1995-2010.

If debt is at the limit and the extraordinary actions are exhausted, Treasury may not issue debt without further action from Congress and could be forced to delay payments until sufficient funds become available. In the past, Congress and the Secretary of the Treasury have taken additional actions beyond those described above when necessary to ensure that the government paid its obligations as they came due without breaching the debt limit. For example, in 1996, Congress passed and the President signed legislation allowing Treasury to issue securities temporarily excluded from the debt limit in an amount equal to the March 1996 Social Security payments to ensure that benefit payments were made on time.[9]

Treasury has never been unable to pay interest or principal on debt held by the public because of the debt limit. Treasury, credit rating agencies, and others agree that failure to pay principal or interest on Treasury securities because of the debt limit could have costly consequences for the U.S. government and financial markets including higher future borrowing costs for Treasury and the public; stress on the value of the dollar in currency markets; and major disruptions in capital markets due to the repricing of products, services, and transactions dependent on an efficiently functioning Treasury market.

## Increased Borrowing and Limited Borrowing Capacity Provided by Extraordinary Actions Create Debt Management Challenges

### Extraordinary Actions Provide Less Borrowing Capacity Relative to Borrowing Needs than They Did in the Past

The borrowing capacity provided by the extraordinary actions has grown in size but has not kept pace with the growth in Treasury's borrowing needs. The amount potentially provided by the extraordinary actions for a 1-month DISP in fiscal year 2010 was less than the monthly increase in debt subject to the limit for most months of the year. As of August 31, 2010, the extraordinary actions available to Treasury could provide about $147.5 billion in additional borrowing capacity without a DISP and an additional $7.7 billion per month based on the length of the DISP declared. As table 2 shows, the amounts available from suspending G-Fund investments, suspending ESF investments and the disinvestment of CSRDF funds have all grown—with the bulk of the growth in the G-Fund. G-Fund growth results from an increase in federal employee retirement funds being invested in Treasury securities. However, the estimated total borrowing capacity provided by extraordinary actions available without a DISP is still $15 billion below Treasury's average monthly borrowing needs in fiscal year 2010, which was over $162 billion, and only 44 percent of the largest single monthly increase in debt subject to the limit, which was over $330 billion. Treasury officials stated that there are no additional

**Table 2. Estimated Borrowing Capacity Provided by Extraordinary Actions**

| Dollars in billions | | | | |
|---|---|---|---|---|
| | | Fiscal year | | |
| **Extraordinary action** | **2002** | **2005** | **2006** | **2010** |
| **Extraordinary actions that do not require the declaration of a DISP** | | | | |
| Exchanging FFB debt for debt that is subject to the limit[a] | $0.0 | $1.0 | $1.0 | $4.8 |
| Suspension of G-Fund investments | 44.0 | 62.6 | 72.2 | 122.3 |
| Suspension of ESF investments | 9.8 | 15.2 | 15.6 | 20.4 |
| **Subtotal—extraordinary actions available without declaring a DISP** | **$53.8** | **$78.8** | **$88.8** | **$147.5** |
| **Extraordinary actions that require the declaration of a DISP (amount per month** | | | | |
| Suspension of new CSRDF investments[b] | 1.7 | 2.0 | 2.1 | 2.0 |
| Disinvestment of securities held by the CSRDF | 4.0 | 4.6 | 4.8 | 5.7 |
| **Total** | **$59.6** | **$85.3** | **$95.8** | **$155.2** |

Source: GAO and Department of the Treasury.

Notes: These estimates represent an approximation of the additional borrowing capacity provided by the extraordinary actions as of August 31st of each year—the last month in the fiscal year for which data are typical of most months of the year. They do not reflect the actual amount of borrowing capacity Treasury obtained by taking extraordinary actions in any given year.

[a] Some or all of the $15 billion in FFB 9(a) securities that FFB can issue were already exchanged for debt subject to the limit.

[b] Treasury can also suspend large investments to the CSRDF that are made three times a year. In June and December, Treasury makes semiannual interest payments to the CSRDF and in September, Treasury makes a onetime investment in the CSRDF for financing the unfunded liability of new and increased annuity benefits. These amounts would be added to the monthly averages calculated above.

Some of the options used in the past are either more limited or no longer available. FFB has the authority to issue up to $15 billion in securities that are not subject to the debt limit that it can exchange for other Treasury securities to reduce the amount of debt subject to the limit. However, some or all of these FFB securities may be outstanding from previous transactions, including those made to manage the amount of debt subject to the limit in the past, and therefore unavailable. For example, as of August 31, 2010, the exchange of FFB securities for other Treasury securities could provide less than $5 billion in additional borrowing capacity under the debt limit. In the past, FFB reversed these transactions by redeeming FFB 9(a) obligations prior to maturity once the debt limit was raised. However, Treasury officials said they no longer reverse these transactions because of the potential costs FFB and its counterparties could incur as a result.[10] Also, until March 2004, Treasury kept "compensating balances" in non-interest-bearing accounts at banks to compensate them for collecting federal receipts for the Treasury. This allowed Treasury to call back tens of billions of dollars when needed to pay obligations and avoid breaching the debt limit.[11] Since these compensating balances were replaced in March 2004 by direct payment to banks for services, this option is no longer available.

Assuming current borrowing trends, our estimates show that the borrowing capacity provided by the extraordinary actions would be sufficient to meet the government's borrowing needs for as little as a few days to a few weeks during certain times of the year. This means that once debt approaches the debt limit, Treasury may not be able to manage the amount of debt subject to the limit for as long a period of time as it had in the past before the debt limit must be increased or payments must be delayed. Figure 2 below shows the estimated borrowing capacity provided by these actions for a 1-month DISP relative to the monthly change in debt subject to the limit for fiscal year 2010 and 3 previous fiscal years in which Treasury took extraordinary actions. The amount potentially provided by the extraordinary actions for a 1-month DISP in fiscal year 2010 was less than the monthly increase in debt subject to the limit in 8 of the 12 months. In contrast, in earlier years, the potential borrowing capacity provided by the extraordinary actions was greater than the monthly increase in debt subject to the limit in almost all months.

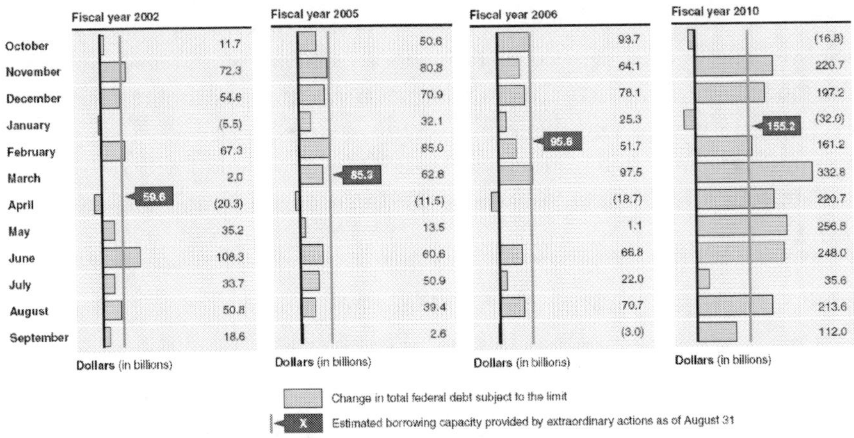


Source: GAO analysis of Treasury data.

Figure 2. Estimated Borrowing Capacity Provided by Extraordinary Actions Based on a 1-Month DISP Relative to Actual Monthly Changes in Debt Subject to the Limit for Select Years.

The actions available without declaration of a DISP could potentially provide $147.5 billion (as of Aug. 31, 2010), but the amount of time that these actions provide before debt reaches the limit depends on a number of factors. For instance, debt subject to the limit increases sharply certain days of the year. Treasury makes semiannual interest payments on a large amount of debt held in government accounts on the last day of June and December.[12] During the recent debt limit debate in early fiscal year 2010, debt increased by more than $165 billion in a single day—December 31— because of $81 billion in net nonmarketable securities issuances, including interest payments to government accounts,[13] as well as $84 billion in net marketable securities issuances.

Another factor that determines the amount of time that Treasury is able to manage debt near the debt limit is the size of Treasury's operating cash balance. Treasury can draw down its operating cash balance to pay obligations rather than increase borrowing. While the size of Treasury's operating cash balance routinely fluctuates throughout the year depending on the timing of withdrawals and deposits, table 3 shows that Treasury's average operating cash balance was roughly twice as high in fiscal year 2009 and fiscal year 2010 as it was in the previous 6 fiscal years. From December 15, 2009, to February 11, 2010, when debt was approaching the debt limit, Treasury's operating cash balance (excluding the SFP account balance) rarely fell below

$90 billion.[14] Higher cash balances helped ensure that Treasury had enough cash available to make large disbursements on short notice. Treasury officials explained that higher cash balances were not related to the debt limit but rather to regular and predictable financing patterns coupled with large receipts and expenditures related to the Troubled Asset Relief Program (TARP), Recovery Act, and other legislation to address the financial crisis and the economic downturn.

**Table 3. Average Operating Cash Balance Less Supplementary Financing Program Account Balance, Fiscal Years 2003-2010**

| Dollars in billions | | | | | | | | |
|---|---|---|---|---|---|---|---|---|
| **Fiscal year** | **2003** | **2004** | **2005** | **2006** | **2007** | **2008** | **2009** | **2010** |
| Average operating cash balance | 17.9 | 20.5 | 25.9 | 26.4 | 30.6 | 24.9 | 58.9 | 57.7 |

Source: GAO analysis of Treasury data.

The amount of additional borrowing capacity provided by disinvesting CSRDF securities depends on the length of the DISP declared by the Secretary.[15] For past DISPs, the Secretary determined the amount of disinvestments based on the length of the DISP and the estimated monthly CSRDF benefit payments that would occur during this time. For example, Treasury declared a DISP from May 16 to June 28, 2002, and disinvested about $4 billion in Treasury securities held by the CSRDF. This amount was roughly equal to the amount that would have been needed to make 1 month's worth of Civil Service benefit payments. Similarly, Treasury declared a 12-month DISP in November 1995 and disinvested $39.8 billion in Treasury securities held by the CSRDF, roughly the equivalent of 12 months' worth of benefit payments. The statute does not require that disinvestments be made only for the purpose of making CSRDF benefit payments. However, Treasury cannot disinvest additional securities later to make those benefit payments. As a result, the amount provided by the CSRDF declines over the period of the DISP. In the past 16 years, the Secretary of the Treasury declared DISPs ranging from 14 days to 14 months. The period of time between the declaration of a DISP and the debt limit increase ranged from 1 day to 4-$^{1/2}$ months.

## Treasury Diverts Resources from Other Priorities to Manage Debt near the Limit

Debt and cash management require more time and Treasury resources as debt nears the debt limit. The size and timing of auctions must be adjusted when nearing the debt limit; cash and borrowing needs must be forecasted and monitored with increasing frequency and in increasing detail; and contingency plans and alternative scenarios for the possible implementation of extraordinary actions must be developed, reviewed, and tested. These activities divert time and Treasury resources from other cash and debt management issues. We reviewed estimates provided by the Office of Debt Management (ODM), the Office of Fiscal Projections (OFP), and the Bureau of the Public Debt (BPD) that overall indicated they devoted as much as several hundred hours per week to managing debt near the debt limit.

Treasury's operational focus on the debt limit begins as early as 6 to 9 months before the debt limit is expected to be reached and increases as debt nears the limit. Since this work involves contingency planning, it is undertaken whether or not the debt limit is raised prior to the use of extraordinary actions or the declaration of a DISP. For example, Treasury staff develop projections under multiple scenarios of when debt might reach the debt limit. As debt nears the debt limit, these projections and scenarios are developed weekly, then daily, and finally as often as multiple times a day. According to Treasury, these projections and scenarios may take 3 of OFP's 11 staff members between 2 to 4 hours per day to produce.

While Treasury needs accurate cash-flow forecasts to project changes in the amount of debt subject to the limit, the precision and frequency increases when debt is near or at the limit. While large regular and predictable payments and receipts—such as Medicare and Social Security payments and receipts from corporate taxes—cause predictable swings in daily deposits and withdrawals, an official from OFP said that it was uncertainty about other revenue and irregular payments that made planning and forecasting more difficult as debt approached the debt limit in fiscal year 2010. For example, as figure 3 shows, Treasury received an influx of repayments of more than $90 billion from financial institutions under TARP in December 2009. However, since Treasury did not know for certain when these payments would be received, Treasury officials ran multiple projections of when the debt limit would be reached.

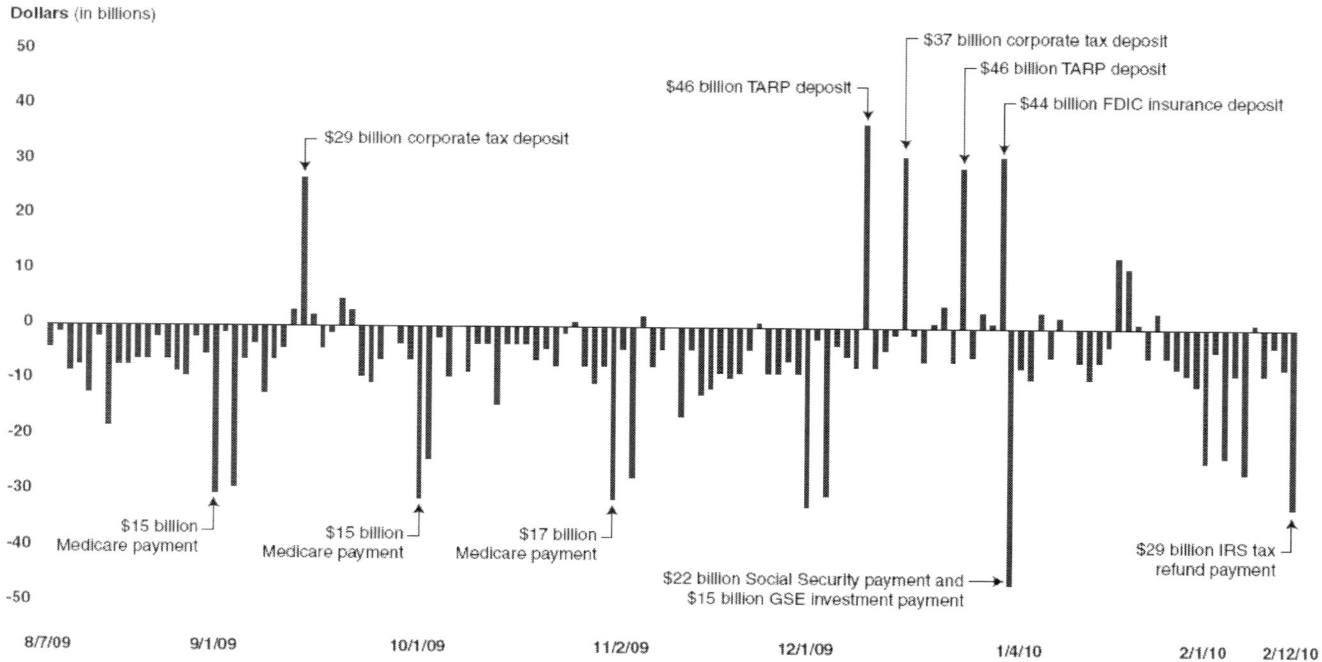


Source: GAO analysis of Treasury data.

Note: Net cash flow is equal to deposits less withdrawals. This excludes federal debt transactions including noncash transactions involving debt held in government accounts such as large regularly occurring interest payments in late December.

Figure 3. Daily Change in Net Cash Flows during Recent Debt Limit Event Period, August 7, 2009, to February 12, 2010.

Treasury uses the projections of debt subject to the limit not only for operational scenarios but also in meetings to inform senior Treasury officials—including the Secretary. These meetings also increase in frequency from monthly to as often as daily as debt approaches the limit. The meetings, which have included 10 or more executives and senior career staff, are used to discuss strategies for managing debt near the debt limit including the potential use of extraordinary actions. According to Treasury, these meetings can require several hours of preparation. While Treasury officials and staff can draw on previous experiences managing debt near the debt limit, they told us that each debt limit event presents new and different issues to be considered and addressed; in addition, there are often senior officials who have not been through the experience and must be fully briefed and prepared.

BPD—the bureau within Treasury that is responsible for implementing the extraordinary actions and the accounting associated with those transactions—also dedicates extensive resources on operations related to the debt limit. BPD estimates that a 2-month DISP results in roughly 1,900 hours of work including the time spent before, during, and after the debt limit increase. This includes more than 400 hours in the 6 weeks prior to the implementation of any extraordinary actions spent on meetings to prepare for when the debt limit is reached, preparation of parallel accounts and spreadsheets in the event that extraordinary actions involving the G-Fund and CSRDF are used, tests of the accounting system, and a mock auction to practice and verify procedures for potential auction postponements. BPD also estimates that it spends in excess of 140 hours on debt limit–related activities each week once the first extraordinary action is taken, and over 270 hours on activities such as unwinding past transactions and preparing reports after the debt limit has been increased. The increased workload could result in overtime hours for BPD employees.

Treasury officials said that the increased focus on debt limit–related operations in the months and weeks approaching the debt limit can divert time and attention from other tasks that could improve Treasury operations. For example, according to Treasury, OFP is able to spend less time working to update or improve the models it uses in routine forecasting of tax receipts, expenditures, and borrowing needs. Similarly, Treasury officials said that ODM is able to spend less time analyzing short-term financing needs that could help inform auction amounts. Both of these activities help Treasury more accurately project future borrowing needs to avoid the following:

(1) Borrowing more than is needed to fund the government's immediate needs, which results in increased interest costs.

(2) Borrowing less than is sufficient to maintain Treasury's operating cash balance at a minimum level through regularly scheduled issuances of marketable Treasury securities. This may require Treasury to issue CM bills with little advance notice to the market, resulting in potentially higher interest costs for the federal government.

## APPROACHING THE DEBT LIMIT CAN ADD UNCERTAINTY IN THE TREASURY MARKET

### Postponed Auctions and Other Disruptions May Lead to Increased Borrowing Costs

Some of the actions Treasury takes to manage the amount of debt as it approaches the debt limit disrupt the regular and predictable auction schedule that Treasury relies on to promote liquid markets and finance the government's borrowing needs at the lowest cost over time. Regular and predictable auctions provide investors greater certainty and better information with which to plan their investments. Meanwhile, a liquid market allows investors to more easily buy and sell Treasury securities in the secondary market. Market participants that we spoke with said that any actions that Treasury takes to manage debt as it approaches the limit that cause Treasury to deviate from its otherwise regular and predictable schedule or reduce liquidity introduce uncertainty into the Treasury market and have the potential to increase Treasury's borrowing costs.

Since 1995, Treasury delayed the announcement of 17 regularly scheduled auctions by 1-1/2 hours to 7 business days and postponed the auction date for 11 auctions by as many as 8 business days (see table 4). Treasury also reduced the offering size of a 13-week bill by $7 billion after the initial auction announcement in October 1995 in order to stay under the debt limit. These actions introduced uncertainty into the market for Treasury securities, and in some circumstances may have increased borrowing costs.

## Table 4. Postponed Auctions and Delayed Auction Announcements, 1995-2010

| Type of Security | Originally scheduled announcement date | Date of actual auction announcement | Original auction date | Actual auction date | Length of delay in announcement (business days) | Length of auction postponement (business days) |
|---|---|---|---|---|---|---|
| 3-year note | 11/1/1995 | 11/13/1995 | 11/7/1995 | 11/20/1995 | 7 | 8 |
| 10-year note | 11/1/1995 | 11/13/1995 | 11/8/1995 | 11/21/1995 | 7 | 8 |
| 52-week bill | 11/2/1995 | 11/13/1995 | 11/9/1995 | 11/15/1995 | 6 | 3 |
| 2-year note | 6/19/2002 | 6/28/2002 | 6/26/2002 | 6/28/2002 | 7 | 2 |
| 13-week bill | 6/27/2002 | 6/28/2002 | 7/1/2002 | 7/1/2002 | 1 | 0 |
| 26-week bill | 6/27/2002 | 6/28/2002 | 7/1/2002 | 7/1/2002 | 1 | 0 |
| 13-week bill | 5/15/2003 | 5/19/2003 | 5/19/2003 | 5/20/2003 | 2 | 1 |
| 26-week bill | 5/15/2003 | 5/19/2003 | 5/19/2003 | 5/20/2003 | 2 | 1 |
| 4-week bill | 5/19/2003 | 5/19/2003 | 5/20/2003 | 5/21/2003 | — | 1 |
| 13-week bill | 5/22/2003 | 5/27/2003 | 5/27/2003 | 5/28/2003 | 2 | 1 |
| 26-week bill | 5/22/2003 | 5/27/2003 | 5/27/2003 | 5/28/2003 | 2 | 1 |
| 2-year note | 5/22/2003 | 5/27/2003 | 5/28/2003 | 5/29/2003 | 2 | 1 |

**Table 4. (Continued).**

| Type of Security | Originally scheduled announcement date | Date of actual auction announcement | Original auction date | Actual auction date | Length of delay in announcement (business days) | Length of auction postponement (business days) |
|---|---|---|---|---|---|---|
| 4-week bill | 11/15/2004 | 11/19/2004 | 11/16/2004 | 11/19/2004 | 4 | 3 |
| 13-week bill | 11/18/2004 | 11/19/2004 | 11/22/2004 | 11/22/2004 | 1 | 0 |
| 26-week bill | 11/18/2004 | 11/19/2004 | 11/22/2004 | 11/22/2004 | 1 | 0 |
| 2-year note | 11/18/2004 | 11/19/2004 | 11/23/2004 | 11/23/2004 | 1 | 0 |
| 13-week bill | 3/16/2006 | 3/16/2006 | 3/20/2006 | 3/20/2006 | 0[a] | 0 |
| 26-week bill | 3/16/2006 | 3/16/2006 | 3/20/2006 | 3/20/2006 | 0[a] | 0 |

Source: GAO analysis of Treasury data.

[a]Treasury's auction announcement release time was delayed from 11:00 a.m. to 12:30 p.m.

Treasury officials and market participants both stated that postponing the announcement or auction of longer-dated securities such as notes and bonds is more disruptive to the Treasury market than postponing shorter-dated securities such as bills. This is due in part to the fact that dealers generally require additional time to work with customers and secure financing for note and bond auctions. There is generally about a week between the announcement of a note auction and the actual auction. The announcement of a 2-year note auction was delayed 7 business days in 2002, reducing the time that dealers had to prepare bids from 5 business days to less than 1. This auction had the lowest bid-to-cover ratio—the ratio of dollar value of bids at auction to the amount accepted—for any 2- year note auction since these data began to be recorded in 1998. It is difficult to say with certainty how much in additional interest Treasury paid because of the postponement of this auction. Based on one estimate that assumes that the rate on the note would have been roughly equal to the constant maturity rate, or the closing rate on actively traded Treasury securities maturing at the same time on the day that the auction actually took place, Treasury paid an additional 7 basis points—or 0.07 percentage points—on the $27 billion in 2-year notes issued that day. This equals almost $19 million in additional interest costs each year. Based on an alternative estimate that assumes that Treasury would have received the prevailing interest rate on 2-year notes in the secondary market on the day that the auction was originally scheduled to take place, the increased interest costs would be even greater.

The level of disruption resulting from a postponed auction depends in part on how early Treasury forewarns the market. Unlike the 2-year note auction in 2002, Treasury discussed the prospect of postponing a 3-year note and a 10-year note auction with members of the Treasury Borrowing Committee at its regular committee meeting a week before the original auction date and released the auction announcement a week before the postponed auction took place. The yields at the subsequent auctions on November 20 and 21, 1995 were roughly the same as the constant maturity rate for each maturity on the day of the auction.

Auctions that are postponed beyond the maturity date of a previously issued security can cause significant disruptions. Treasury generally makes the actual exchange of Treasury securities for cash—the settlement—a few days or more after the auction. Settlements frequently occur around the same time that previously issued securities are maturing. This allows Treasury to refund maturing securities—to use some or all of the cash that it raised in the auction to redeem maturing securities. It also allows investors to easily roll over, or reinvest, cash received from maturing securities in newly issued securities. Treasury stated that when the settlement date of a new security is moved past the maturity date of a previously issued security, investors are unable to rollover their investments in a timely way. As a result, they may choose to invest in a financial instrument other than Treasury securities. This could affect auction demand. Most of the postponed auctions in the past 16 years were delayed by only 1 to 3 days and therefore did not affect the refunding of maturing securities. However, in November 1995, the 3- and 10-year note auctions intended to refund notes maturing on November 15, 1995, were postponed past the maturity date. In this instance, Treasury bridged the gap between the maturity and settlement date by auctioning a short-term CM bill.

Overall, Treasury issued 20 CM bills totaling more than $300 billion during DISPs in the past 16 years to manage the amount of debt near the limit. In some cases, these were used to augment Treasury's regular schedule of bill auctions. For example, because of debt limit constraints, Treasury delayed the 4-week bill auction scheduled for November 16, 2004. Treasury then auctioned a 5-day CM bill for $7 billion on November 17, 2004. As mentioned previously, our prior work found that Treasury may have paid a premium, in the form of higher interest, on these CM bills compared to bills of a similar maturity.[16]

## Treasury Sharply Reduced the Supply of Bills during Recent Debt Limit Debate

While Treasury did not postpone any of its regularly scheduled auctions during the most recent debt limit debate, it sharply reduced the total dollar amount of bills outstanding primarily to manage the amount of debt as it approached the limit. The total amount of Treasury bills outstanding dropped by $350 billion (or about 17 percent) from September 23, 2009, to February 12, 2010, (see fig. 4). Roughly $200 billion of this was related to reductions to the SFP. The decline in Treasury bills outstanding was accompanied by a decline in short-term rates paid by Treasury. However, Treasury officials and market participants stated that a sharp and irregular bill reduction in such a short period of time could affect liquidity in the near term and add uncertainty in the market over the longer term. While several different types of investors use bills to invest their funds in the short term in a safe and highly liquid asset, market participants we spoke with said that money market funds were likely most affected by the reduction in bill supply.

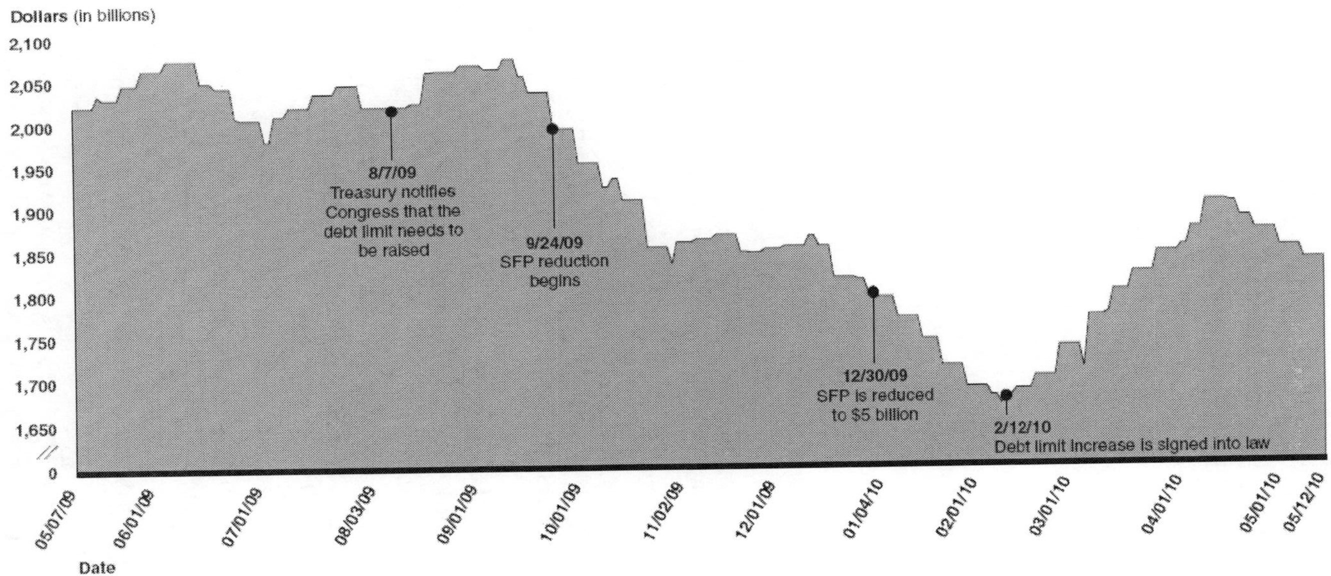


Source: GAO analysis of Treasury data.

Figure 4. Supply of Treasury  Bills Decreased Sharply during Debt Limit Event.

Market participants also noted that if Treasury had to make similar reductions to its issuance of notes or bonds because of proximity to the debt limit, the effect on the Treasury market would be greater.

This sharp reduction in Treasury bills was unique to this most-recent debt limit debate and largely related to the SFP, though large TARP repayments in December, a reduction in Treasury's operating cash balance, and the transition to longer-dated securities were also factors. When Treasury approached the debt limit earlier in the decade, the amount of Treasury bills outstanding tended to fluctuate within a narrower range. To finance the SFP program, Treasury auctions a series of CM bills, and places the proceeds in a special account at the Federal Reserve Bank of New York. These outstanding CM bills count against the debt limit. On September 16, 2009, Treasury announced it intended to reduce the SFP account from $200 billion to $15 billion to preserve flexibility in debt management. This amount dropped to as low as zero in December 2009. As late as February 2, 2010, Treasury announced that both the outlook for Treasury bills issuance and the future of the SFP were uncertain. Shortly after the debt limit was raised on February 12, 2010, Treasury returned the SFP account to approximately $200 billion.

## Evidence Suggests Borrowing Costs Increased during Some Debt Limit Event Periods

Our analysis suggests that the general uncertainty surrounding some debt limit events including the most recent in 2009-2010 increased Treasury's borrowing costs in the months immediately prior to a debt limit increase.[17] To measure changes in Treasury's borrowing costs, we examined the spread between 13-week (i.e., 3-month) Treasury bill yields and 3-month commercial paper yields around debt limit events since 2001.[18] Rates for Treasury bills, commercial paper, and other financial assets can fluctuate from day to day in response to changes in the broader economy. By focusing on a yield spread rather than changes in individual interest rates, we are able to better measure changes in the relative risk of 3-month Treasury bills and identify potential risk premiums. A narrowing of the spread indicates that the market perceives the risk of Treasury bills to be closer to that of commercial paper, while a widening of this spread means that Treasury bills are perceived to be less risky relative to commercial paper. We found that Treasury paid a premium on 3-month

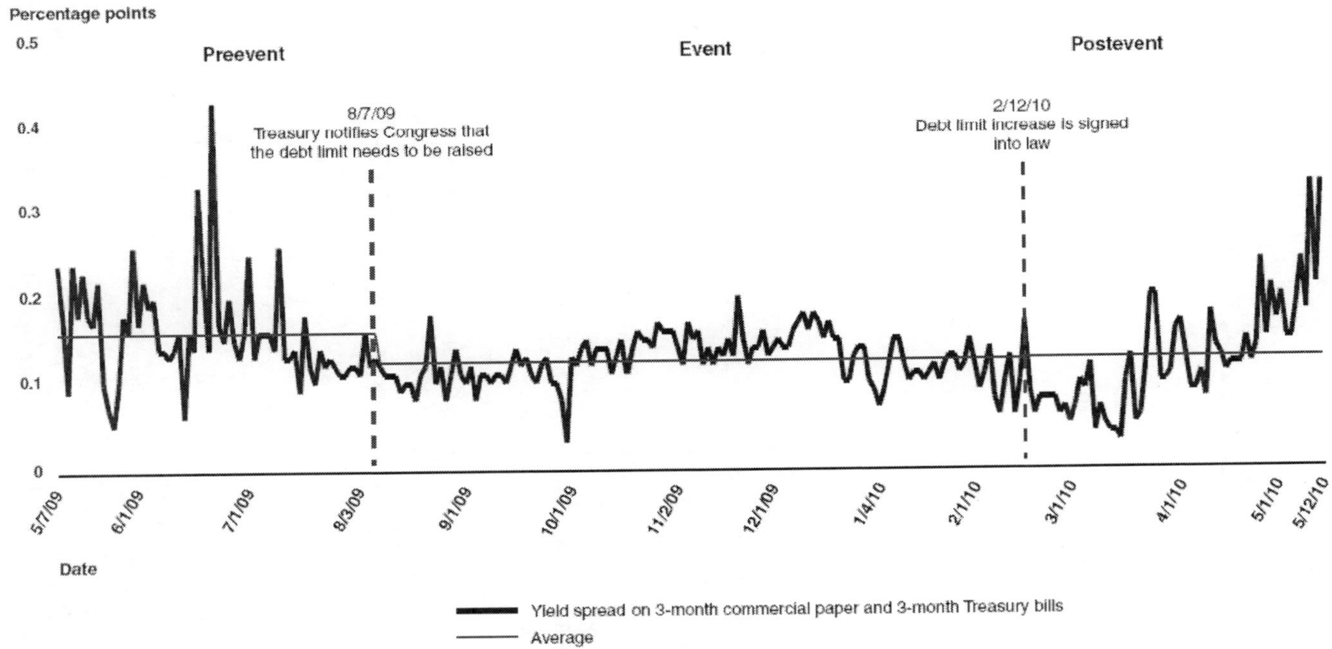


Source: GAO analysis of Board of Governors of the Federal Reserve System data.

Figure 5. Spreads between Yields of 3-Month Commercial Paper and 3-Month Treasury Bills Were Lower during the 2009–2010 Debt Limit Event Period.

Treasury bills issued during debt limit events in 2001–2002 and 2002–2003, but not in 2004–2005 and 2005–2006.[19] For the most-recent debt limit event—which lasted from August 7, 2009, to February 12, 2010—we found that Treasury again paid a premium on 3-month Treasury bills. Figure 5 shows that the average spread narrowed during the debt limit event in 2009–2010 compared to the average for the proceeding 3 months, implying that Treasury paid a premium on 3-month Treasury bills issued during this time period.

After controlling for other factors that could have affected the yield spread, such as economic uncertainty and liquidity in the bill market, we estimated that the debt limit added a premium of about 4 basis points during the debt limit event period in 2009–2010.[20] Applying this premium to all 3-month Treasury bills issued during this period, we estimate that Treasury paid $78 million in additional borrowing costs as a result of the debt limit. We did not estimate the effects of nearing the debt limit on yields of other Treasury securities, and therefore, do not know whether a premium of the same size would apply to Treasury securities with longer or shorter terms to maturity. However, even a smaller premium on the large amount of Treasury securities issued during the debt limit event period would result in a notable increase in borrowing costs. For instance, for each additional basis point paid on bills issued during the 2009–2010 debt limit event period, Treasury's borrowing cost would increase by roughly $92 million. For more information on our statistical analysis, including a discussion of the limitations, see appendix II.

Trends in U.S. credit default swap (CDS) premia, or "spreads" also suggest that Treasury securities were perceived to be relatively more risky as debt approached the limit in 2009-2010. While CDS are used in a variety of ways other than to insure against a default, such as hedging against counterparty risk, or the risk that another party will not fulfill its contractual obligation, CDS spreads serve as an indicator of changes in the market's perception of risk in the Treasury market. U.S. CDS spreads increase when risk in the Treasury market increases and therefore have an inverse relationship to the yield spread. Not long after Treasury notified Congress that the debt limit would need to be raised and Treasury began reducing issuance of CM bills for the SFP, rates for 1-year U.S. CDS spreads increased while the yield spread trend decreased (see fig. 6). Similarly, in the weeks after the debt limit was raised, U.S. CDS spreads decreased sharply. Some of the increase in U.S. CDS spreads likely reflects general uncertainty about the global economy rather than the debt limit; CDS spreads increased from late 2009 to early 2010 for other countries, not just for the United States.

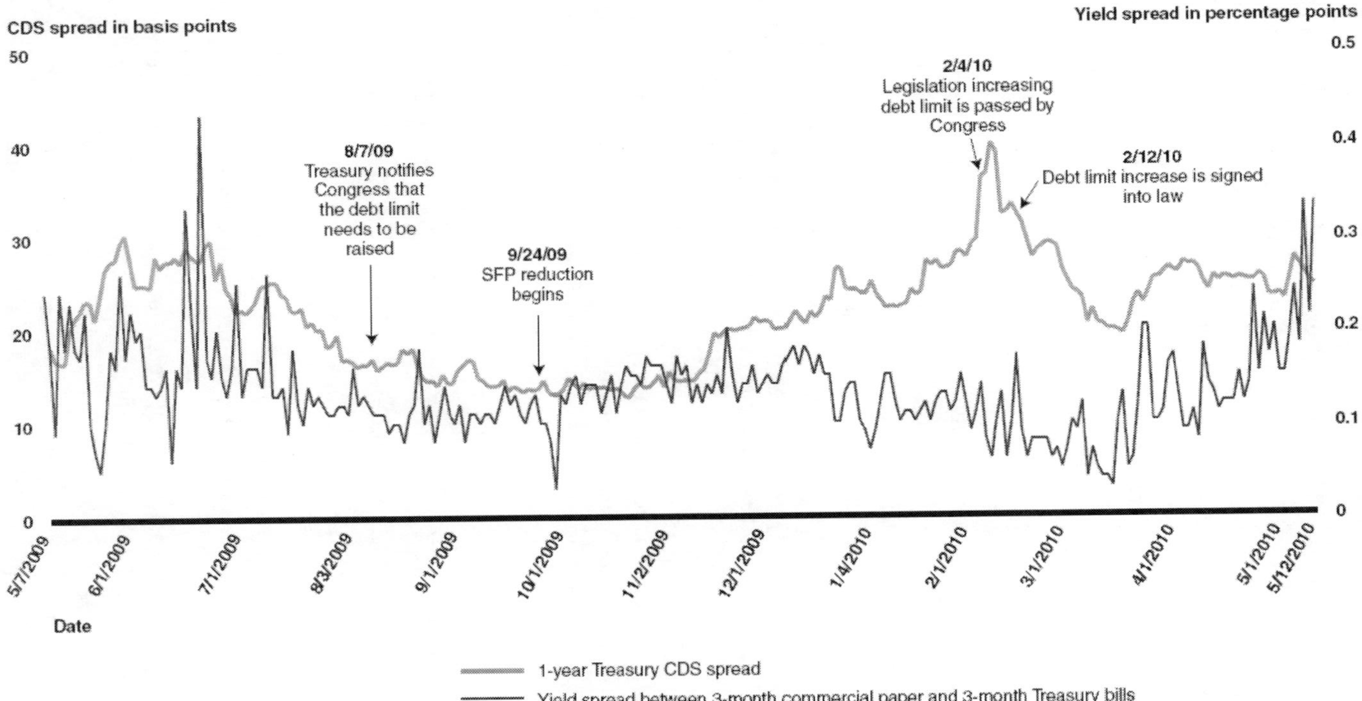


Source: GAO analysis of Board of Governors of the Federal Reserve System data and Datastream data.

Figure 6. Trends in Treasury's CDS Spreads Were Consistent with Trends in the Yield Spread for the 2009–2010 Debt Limit Event.

However, 1-year U.S. CDS spreads tended to increase more than comparable spreads for Germany, Japan, and the United Kingdom during the event period.

Overall, the debt limit requires Treasury to deviate from its regular debt management practices in ways that add uncertainty to the Treasury market. While there are limitations to our analysis of changes to the auction schedule and to Treasury yields around debt limit events, collectively the analyses provide strong evidence that this uncertainty does not come without a cost.

Beyond the immediate costs associated with the debt limit, some market participants and others that we spoke with said that failing to raise the debt limit in a timely manner added an additional level of risk to the Treasury market. As noted above, the extraordinary actions provide less borrowing capacity and therefore less time for debate about raising the debt limit once debt reaches the limit than they have in the past. Analysts and observers—including former congressional staff—expressed concern that a miscalculation in when the debt limit needs to be increased by could trigger a financial crisis in the Treasury market. Despite these concerns, most of those whom we spoke with believe that Congress will raise the debt limit before there is a significant market disruption and that Treasury will continue to successfully manage debt near the debt limit as it has done in the past. Treasury continues to consistently borrow at relatively low interest rates, and demand for Treasury securities both in the United States and abroad remains strong during periods of economic instability because of their liquidity and low risk.

## Experts and Practices of Other Countries Offer Insights for Better Linking Policy Decisions with Their Effect on Debt

### Tying Debt Limit Increases to Annual Budget Decisions Is Similar to a Practice Used in Some Other Countries

We spoke with participants, observers, analysts, and other experts representing a range of backgrounds and political perspectives—including former congressional staff, former CBO Directors, former Treasury officials, and representatives from credit rating agencies—about the role of the debt limit in the U.S. budget process. Many cited the failure to link fiscal policy decisions to changes in the debt limit as a weakness in the process. Credit rating agencies, for example, consider a number of different factors when assigning a credit rating to sovereign nations' debt, including the strength of the national economy, overall levels of government debt, and monetary policy, as well as the budgetary framework. While the debt limit has not compromised the United States' AAA credit rating, credit rating agencies expressed concern about separating the vote for spending increases and revenue decreases that increase debt from the vote for additional borrowing authority. One credit rating agency described this delinking as a weakness in the U.S. budgetary framework.[21] Another credit rating agency said that anything that has the potential to delay the timely redemption of federal debt is viewed as a negative.[22] In 1996, Moody's Investors Service (Moody's) indicated a possible downgrade for some Treasury securities with interest payments coming due in part because Treasury had nearly exhausted its options for managing debt near the debt limit. According to Moody's this was the only time that Moody's has officially taken a negative rating action related to U.S. Treasury securities. None of the experts that we spoke with said that the existence of the debt limit served to restrain spending and tax decisions prior to the debt limit debate, but some believe the debt limit has served a useful purpose in highlighting the growth of federal debt.

Many of the experts that we spoke with identified possible changes to the legislative process that would better link decisions about fiscal policy and debt. Some suggested that since the budget resolution reflects aggregate fiscal policy decisions, it should be used to consider the level of debt implied by those decisions. The budget resolution generally sets out the level for spending, revenues, and debt for the next fiscal year and the following 4 fiscal years. Some favored a mechanism similar to what was House Rule XXVIII in the 111th Congress. This rule provided for the automatic engrossment and transmittal to the Senate of a joint resolution changing the debt limit by the amount specified in the budget resolution. This joint resolution was considered to have passed the House and was then sent to the Senate. The Senate did not have a similar rule; it sometimes, though not always, passed the joint resolution from the House, albeit with a lag. In the last 16 years, this lag has ranged from 1 month to more than 10 months. Others believed that this process still gave too little visibility to the implications of spending and tax decisions on federal debt and preferred separate votes on stand-alone legislation. They too believed that the vote should be timed to go with the budget resolution—in part to keep the link and in part to avoid reaching the debt limit later in the year after the spending and tax decisions had been made.

Opinions varied on how to address increases in borrowing needs not contemplated in budget resolutions. The actual amount of debt can differ from the amount anticipated in the budget resolution because of newly enacted legislation or because of the automatic stabilizers through which changes in the economy affect government spending and revenue.[23] Some supported a formal or informal process whereby any legislation that would increase debt beyond that envisioned in the resolution would contain a separate title raising the debt limit by the appropriate amount. Congress took this approach with three pieces of legislation enacted in 2008 and 2009 in response to the financial market crisis and economic downturn. The Housing and Economic Recovery Act of 2008, the Emergency Economic Stabilization Act of 2008, and the Recovery Act each included a separate provision increasing the debt limit. Some congressional observers pointed out that while this would tie spending and revenue decisions to the debt-level effect of those decisions, it would not address increases in debt arising from an economic downturn. Some of the ideas for dealing with both the policy linkage and any increases in debt driven by economic conditions were (1) considering further changes to the debt limit at the time that the annual mid-session review is released;[24] (2) setting aside a reserve fund in the budget resolution for unanticipated borrowing needs; and (3) delegating additional authority to Treasury to borrow for intrayear financing needs that resulted from changes in the economy rather than direct policy decisions.

The practice of approving borrowing authority in connection with approval of the annual budget is used in other countries we examined. For example, in Canada, the Ministry of Finance is provided with a fixed amount that it is authorized to borrow for the fiscal year. When necessary, the Ministry of Finance can request increased borrowing authority from the executive branch of government to fund unforeseen borrowing needs. In Sweden, the legislature approves borrowing authority annually; however, it is limited to purpose—to finance current deficits, provide loans, and redeem national debt, for example—rather than by amount.

## Some Suggested Delegating Broader Authority to Treasury—a Practice Used in Some Other Countries

Some budget experts and a former Treasury official said that Congress could delegate authority to Treasury to borrow as needed to fund congressionally approved expenditures subject to a periodic review. They suggested that Congress could vote to renew this authority at the start of a new Congress or a new legislative session. This would preserve Congress's ability to have periodic debates over the current path of federal debt, they argue, but change the trigger for debate from proximity to the debt limit to another point in the legislative process to minimize disruptions to debt management and the Treasury market.

Providing finance departments with broad authority to borrow is consistent with practices in four of the countries we examined. In the United Kingdom, for example, the Treasury is given broad authority to raise money in a manner it "considers expedient for the purpose of promoting sound monetary conditions." In New Zealand, the Minister of Finance is given similarly broad borrowing authority to borrow in the public interest. However, when comparing borrowing authority across countries, it is important to recognize that the division of power between the legislative and executive branches varies among different political systems. In parliamentary systems, the government is generally formed by the political party that has the support of the majority of the parliament; therefore, the interests of the legislative and executive branches are likely more aligned, making the delegation of borrowing authority more of a formality and not a subject of extensive deliberation. Of the countries that we reviewed, only Denmark has a fixed nominal debt limit that is raised through legislation outside the annual budget process comparable to the U.S. debt limit. According to a Danish official, the limit is set high enough that it does not impede debt managers' ability to issue debt.

Some of those with whom we spoke said that tying delegation of borrowing authority to a fixed nominal debt limit creates an action-forcing event that draws attention to the growth in federal debt. They noted that previous debt limit debates provided opportunities for the Congress and the President to consider the implications of past fiscal policy decisions on federal borrowing and sometimes played a role in the enactment of budget process agreements intended to slow the growth of future federal borrowing. For example, debt limit increases were passed jointly with budget controls legislation five times between 1985 and 1997[25]—and again in February 2010 with the reenactment of a statutory pay-as-you-go, or PAYGO, rule.[26] Meanwhile, others said that the debate over debt limit increases played a smaller role in fiscal policy discussions in recent years than it had in the past and expected that the debt limit would not be needed to trigger debate over federal borrowing in the future given the already increasing attention to debt and deficits. In addition, some thought that risks associated with the debates—

such as the potential for Congress to delay or to miscalculate the timing of a debt limit increase given the small amount of borrowing capacity provided by the extraordinary actions—outweighed the benefits.

## Some Countries Have Mechanisms to Increase Attention to or Control over Fiscal Policy Decisions that Lead to an Increase in Debt

The United States is unusual among the countries we reviewed in using the authorization of additional borrowing authority as an occasion to draw attention to past fiscal policy decisions. Other countries that we reviewed generally use fiscal rules or targets to increase attention to or control over fiscal policy decisions that lead to an increase in debt. Fiscal rules generally refer to permanent or multiyear constraints on fiscal policy through simple numerical limits on budgetary aggregates. For example, Switzerland has adopted a constitutional "debt brake" that places a limit on expenditures that is equal to the expected revenue for the year adjusted to reflect the country's place in the current business cycle. Differences between estimated and actual numbers are recorded in a separate account that must by law be reduced if it reaches a certain level. Germany has adopted a "golden rule" limiting net borrowing to the amount of investment spending. Germany also approved a constitutional amendment in 2009 requiring that structural deficits not exceed 0.35 percent of gross domestic product (GDP)—or very close to balance.

Instead of budget constraints, some countries use debt targets to establish an acceptable outcome for policymakers to work toward when making fiscal policy decisions. These can be either statutory requirements or political commitments by the current government. For example, in part to keep debt at a sustainable level, Sweden targets a net surplus of 1 percent of GDP over the course of the business cycle. In New Zealand, the government is required to maintain debt at a "prudent level" and set specific short-term and long-term targets for meeting this goal. If the government deviates from these targets, the Minister of Finance must explain the approach the government intends to take to return to prudent levels. Members of the European Union agreed to target a ratio of gross general government debt to GDP of 60 percent and budget deficits of not more than 3 percent of GDP. Several nations have struggled to meet these targets in recent years, raising concerns about the effectiveness of the current enforcement mechanisms. In general, budget experts and other observers have noted that the success of fiscal rules depends on effective enforcement along with a sustained commitment by policymakers and the public.

Specific fiscal rules and targets used in other countries may not be appropriate for the United States given differences in the national economies and political institutions. Nevertheless, some of the fiscal rules and targets that we reviewed shared some common features that distinguish them from the U.S. debt limit and offer insights for increasing attention to or control over fiscal policy decisions that lead to an increase in debt. These rules and targets

1) measure debt in relation to the overall size of the economy (e.g., debt-to-GDP ratio),
2) take into consideration whether the economy is in a period of expansion or contraction,
3) provide a near-term or medium-term debt target, as opposed to a ceiling, for policymakers to work toward.

In recent years, several bipartisan and nonpartisan groups have suggested the establishment of fiscal rules with one or more of these features in the United States such as a debt-to-GDP target.[27]

## CONCLUSIONS

The debt limit does not control or limit the ability of the federal government to run deficits or incur obligations. Rather, it is a limit on the ability to pay bills incurred. The decisions that create the need to borrow are made separately from—and generally earlier than—the decision about the debt limit. Debates surrounding the debt limit may raise awareness about the federal government's current debt trajectory and also provide Congress with an opportunity to debate the fiscal policy decisions driving that trajectory. However, since this debate generally occurs after tax and spending decisions have been enacted into law, Congress has a narrower range of options to effect an immediate change to fiscal policy decisions and hence to federal debt.

Failure to raise the debt limit could lead to serious negative consequences in the Treasury market and for the ability of the United States to finance federal debt at the lowest cost over time. Any delay in raising the debt limit that affects Treasury's regular and predictable schedule of auctions can create uncertainty in the Treasury market. So too some of the actions Treasury takes to manage the amount of debt near the debt limit, such as reducing the size of auctions, can compromise the certainty of supply that Treasury relies on to achieve the lowest borrowing cost over time. This uncertainty can, in turn, raise the cost of financing the federal debt. In addition, managing debt near the debt limit diverts Treasury's limited resources away from other cash and debt management issues at a time when Treasury already faces significant challenges in lengthening the average maturity of its debt portfolio, which reduces rollover risk and uncertainty about future interest payments.

Recently—and for the foreseeable future—Treasury's actions take place in the context of rapidly growing federal debt. Treasury's past success at managing cash and debt when near or at the debt limit is no guarantee that it can continue to manage successfully in the future and may be misleading. Given the size of current and projected borrowing needs, the extraordinary actions Treasury uses to manage debt near or at the debt limit will be more limited in coming years. As a result, once debt is at the debt limit, Congress will likely have less time to debate raising the debt limit before there are disruptions to government programs and services and to the Treasury market.

Observers and participants with whom we spoke suggested that improving the link between the spending and revenue decisions that increase the need to borrow and changes in the debt limit would improve the situation. Better alignment could be possible if decisions about the debt level occur in conjunction with spending and revenue decisions as opposed to the after-the-fact approach now used. This would help avoid the uncertainty and disruptions that occur during debates on the debt limit today. It might also facilitate efforts to change the fiscal path by highlighting the implications of these spending and revenue decisions on debt. This will be particularly important in coming years as the federal government addresses the challenge of unsustainable increases in federal debt.

## MATTER FOR CONGRESSIONAL CONSIDERATION

The projections of a growing debt burden have raised concerns both in Congress and in the public. Well-designed budget processes and metrics can help as Congress and the President seek to address the federal government's long-term fiscal challenge. The current design of the debt limit does not engender or facilitate debate over specific tax or spending proposals and their effect on debt. In addition, the uncertainty it creates can lead to disruptions in the Treasury market and in turn to higher borrowing costs. To avoid these potential disruptions to the Treasury market and to help inform the fiscal policy debate in a timely way, Congress should consider ways to better link decisions about the debt limit with decisions about spending and revenue. Such a process would build on the approach used in 2008 and 2009 when Congress passed and the President signed three laws that were expected to increase borrowing with a corresponding increase in the debt limit.[28] This report presents a number of approaches that could serve as a basis for better linking decisions about spending and revenue with decisions about the debt limit.

## AGENCY COMMENTS

We requested comments on a draft of this report from the Secretary of the Treasury. Treasury officials told us they appreciated the in-depth and careful analysis contained in the report. They also provided technical comments, which we incorporated as appropriate.

Susan J. Irving
Director for Federal Budget Analysis Strategic Issues

Gary T. Engel
Director
Financial Management and Assurance

## APPENDIX I: OBJECTIVES, SCOPE, AND METHODOLOGY

Our objectives were to (1) describe the actions that the Department of the Treasury (Treasury) has taken to manage debt near the debt limit and challenges that arise, (2) analyze the effects that approaching the debt limit had on the market for Treasury securities, including Treasury's borrowing costs, and (3) in light of the disconnect between the debt limit and the policy decisions that have an effect on the size of federal debt, describe alternative triggers or mechanisms that would permit consideration of the link between policy decisions and the effect on debt when or before decisions are made.

To answer our first objective, we reviewed Treasury documents and prior GAO reports describing the actions that Treasury has taken during debt limit debates since 1995. We used publicly available data including Treasury's

Monthly Statement of Public Debt and federal investment account statements to estimate the amount of potential borrowing capacity these actions could provide in fiscal year 2010 in comparison to previous years since 2002 in which debt approached the debt limit. To identify challenges that might arise when managing debt near the debt limit, we examined publicly available data from the Daily Treasury Statement to identify trends in federal receipts and expenditures, issuance and redemption of federal debt, and changes in Treasury's operating cash balance. To understand how managing debt near the debt limit affected agency operations, we reviewed documents provided by Treasury, interviewed Treasury officials involved in both the decision-making process and implementation of extraordinary actions, and obtained estimates when possible of the time and staff involved in planning for when the debt limit will be reached and implementing the extraordinary actions. To assess the reasonableness of Treasury estimates, we reviewed calendar appointments and other supporting documents. However, we did not obtain sufficient supporting documentation to independently verify Treasury's estimates. We were also unable to independently verify the foregone opportunities that Treasury identified, such as less time to analyze short-term financing needs, in part because it is difficult to prove what would happen in the absence of the debt limit event.

To identify the potential effects of approaching the debt limit on the market for Treasury securities, we reviewed publicly available Treasury documents such as minutes from meetings of the Treasury Borrowing Advisory Committee and academic literature, and interviewed Treasury officials. Our review covered the last 16 years (1995–2010) in order to include a particularly disruptive debt limit debate in 1995–1996 that required Treasury to take a number of extraordinary actions, as well as the experts including six primary dealers for their general views on the effects of delays in raising the debt limit on the market for Treasury securities and Treasury operations.

On the basis of this initial analysis, we performed the following: (1) We used press releases, auction announcements, and historical auction data since 1995 to identify instances when auctions or auction announcements or both, were delayed as a result of the debt limit. We compared the yields at postponed auctions with yields on Treasury securities of the same maturity being sold in the secondary market to estimate the effect of delaying auctions or auction announcements on Treasury's borrowing costs. We discussed our methodology with Treasury officials and staff at the Federal Reserve Bank of New York and incorporated their suggestions and feedback when appropriate. (2) We used data provided by Treasury to analyze changes in the amount of

Treasury bills outstanding during debt limit debates since 2002. (3) We performed a multivariate regression analysis to estimate the effect of the debt limit on Treasury's borrowing costs. See appendix II for more details on our methodology used for estimating these costs and limitations to our analysis. (4) In August 2010, we received written or oral responses to a standard questionnaire from four primary dealers and managers of a large mutual fund asking for their views on postponed auctions, reductions in bills outstanding, Treasury's extraordinary actions, and the general uncertainty related to the timing of debt limit increases. To obtain a broader perspective on the effects of approaching the debt limit on financial markets, we also spoke with representatives from two of the three major rating agencies, a major trade organization representing securities firms and other financial institutions, a research and consulting firm for the municipal bond market, and a State and Local Government Series securities subscriber.

To examine the disconnect between the debt limit and the policy decisions that have an effect on the size of federal debt, we conducted a literature review and reviewed the legislative history of laws increasing the debt limit. We began our review with the debt limit increase enacted on December 12, 1985, because (1) this was the first in a series of debt limit increases enacted in legislation containing budget process reforms, and (2) after 1985, Congress provided Treasury with its current authorities related to the G-Fund and Civil Service Retirement and Disability Fund (CSRDF) thereby changing the way in which Treasury manages debt near or at the debt limit.

To identify and describe alternative triggers or mechanisms that would permit consideration of the link between policy decisions and the effect on debt when or before decisions are made, we reviewed articles in academic journals and reports and other information published by credit rating agencies and policy research organizations. We conducted semistructured interviews with budget and legislative experts. To ensure that we captured a broad range of perspectives, we sought to include a minimum number of representatives from the following categories: former congressional staff with experience working for one or more of relevant committees (i.e., the House Budget Committee, the House Committee on Ways and Means, the Senate Budget Committee, and the Senate Finance Committee) or senior party leadership in the House or Senate; former Congressional Budget Office or Office of Management and Budget Directors; representatives from a broad range of policy research organizations that focus on issues related to the federal debt; and academics and other experts on the legislative process. We interviewed a total of 17 budget and legislative experts representing one or more of these different categories. Five of those interviewed also had experience working at Treasury.

To put U.S. practices into perspective, we examined triggers and mechanisms used by members of the Organisation for Economic Cooperation and Development (OECD)—an international organization comprised of countries committed to democracy and market-based economies. To identify countries for review, we analyzed countries' responses to the 2007 OECD International Database of Budget Practices and Procedures Survey, particularly questions asking about debt, deficit, and other fiscal rules used when developing a budget.[1] We selected countries for further review based on their responses to the survey as well as our review of reports by the OECD and the International Monetary Fund. We sought to include countries that provided a range of different mechanisms for (1) monitoring or controlling debt and (2) delegating borrowing authority from their legislature to debt managers. Our selection was limited to those countries with information on fiscal rules and borrowing authority available in English. We chose seven countries for further review: Canada, Denmark, Germany, New Zealand, Switzerland, Sweden, and the United Kingdom. We contacted representatives from budget offices, debt management offices, or supreme audit institutions in each of these countries for additional information on their respective country's fiscal rules and borrowing authority. While selected countries offer illustrative examples, their experiences are not always applicable to the United States given differences in political systems and economies. In order to assess the reliability of the data used in this report, including proprietary data from Datastream and IHS Global Insight and publicly available data from Treasury and the Federal Reserve, we examined the data to look for outliers and anomalies and, when possible, compared data from multiple sources for consistency. In general, we chose databases that were commonly used by Treasury and researchers to monitor changes in federal debt and related transactions. Where possible and appropriate, we corroborated the results of our data analysis with other sources. On the basis of our assessment, we believe the data are reliable for the purpose of this review.

We conducted our work from December 2009 to January 2011 in accordance with generally accepted government auditing standards. Those standards require that we plan and perform the audit to obtain sufficient, appropriate evidence to provide a reasonable basis for our findings and conclusions based on our audit objectives. We believe that the evidence

[1] See www.oecd.org/gov/budget/database for the results of the survey.

obtained provides a reasonable basis for our findings and conclusions based on our audit objectives.

# APPENDIX II: DETAILED METHODOLOGY AND FINDINGS OF STATISTICAL ANALYSIS OF TREASURY BORROWING COSTS NEAR THE DEBT LIMIT

To measure changes in the Department of the Treasury's (Treasury) borrowing costs when debt is approaching the debt limit, we performed a multivariate regression analysis of yields paid on 13-week (i.e., 3-month) Treasury bills issued during the five debt limit events beginning in fiscal year 2002. For our purposes, a debt limit event begins when the Secretary notifies Congress that the debt limit needs to be raised and ends when legislation increasing the debt limit is signed into law. The dependent variable in our analysis is the spread, or difference, between yields on 3- month Treasury bills and yields on 3-month commercial paper. We used yield spreads during the preevent period 3 months prior to the Secretary's letter as a benchmark against which yields during the event can be compared. A narrowing of the spread indicates that the market perceives the relative risk of Treasury bills to be closer to that of commercial paper, increasing their cost to Treasury. Conversely, a widening of the spread indicates that the market perceives the relative risk of Treasury bills to be less than that of commercial paper, making them less costly to Treasury. We regressed the yield spread on key variables affecting risk and liquidity of the financial market. Our results suggest that Treasury paid a premium ranging from 1 to 4 basis points on 3-month Treasury bills issued during debt limit events in 2001–2002, 2002–2003, and most recently in 2009– 2010.[2] However, we did not observe premiums in 2004–2005 and 2005– 2006.

## Variables and Model Specifications

The existing literature on the effect of the debt limit on Treasury's borrowing costs is limited. Our analysis was based in part on a prior study of the effect of debt limit events on Treasury interest rates by Liu, Shao, and

---

[2] One basis point is equal to 1/100th of 1 percent. Thus, 4 basis points is 0.04 percent.

Yeager.[3] Similar to the results of our analysis, Liu et al. (2009) found that during debt limit events in 2001–2002 and 2002–2003, the spread between 3-month Treasury bill yields and 3-month commercial paper yields narrowed, implying that Treasury bills were relatively more costly during this period; however, this relationship was not observed in either the 2004–2005 or 2005–2006 debt limit events. The authors hypothesized that, during these latter two debt limit events, investors may have assumed based on past experience that members of Congress would resolve their differences before there were any serious disruptions in the Treasury market and therefore did not charge a premium on securities issued near the debt limit. We also reviewed an earlier study by Nippani, Liu, and Schulman which found that Treasury paid a premium on 3-month and 6- month Treasury bills issued during the debt limit event in 1995-1996.[4]

On the basis of discussions with Treasury officials, staff at the Federal Reserve Bank of New York, and market experts such as primary dealers and larger investment funds, we determined that the model developed by Liu et al. (2009) provided a reasonable starting point for our analysis. We made modifications to reflect the Federal Reserve's purchases of commercial paper through its Commercial Paper Funding Facility (CPFF) in 2008 to enhance the liquidity of the commercial paper market. We included a variable to control for the volume of commercial paper held by the Federal Reserve as a percentage of total commercial paper outstanding. We also included the Chicago Board Options Exchange's Volatility Index (VIX) to control for volatility and uncertainty in financial markets. The equation we used is

**Yield Spread = B0 + B1*EVENT + B2*POST + B3*SPRET + B4*VIX + B5*LOG(CPISSUE) + B6*LOG(TBILLTRANS) + B7*CPFFSHARE + Error**

Table 5 below describes each of the variables in the equation and indicates the expected sign of the coefficient. Treasury officials and market experts said that our modifications to their equation were reasonable.

---

[3] Pu Liu, Yingying Shao, and Timothy J. Yeager, "Did the repeated debt ceiling controversies embed default risk in U.S. Treasury securities?" Journal of Banking and Finance, vol. 33 (2009): 1464-1471.

[4] Srinivas Nippani, Pu Liu, and Craig T. Schulman, "Are Treasury Securities Free of Default?" Journal of Financial and Quantitative Analysis, vol. 36, no. 2 (2001): 251-265.

**Table 5. Variables Used in Multivariate Regression**

| Variable name | Variable description |
|---|---|
| EVENT | This variable is equal to 1 during the event period and is 0 otherwise. Consistent with the academic literature, we defined the debt limit event period as beginning when Treasury notified Congress that the debt limit needed to be raised and as ending when the legislation is passed to raise the debt limit. We expect the variable's coefficient to be negative because debt limit events may raise the perceived risk of Treasury securities and reduce the yield spread compared to the preevent period. |
| POST | This variable is equal to 1 in the 3-month postevent period and is otherwise 0. A negative coefficient indicates that the perceived increased risk of Treasury securities persisted beyond the end of the debt limit event period. |
| SPRET | This variable is the daily return of the Standard & Poor's 500 index and is an indicator of the market's assessment of economic activity. We expect the variable's coefficient to be negative because a stronger economy should reduce the default risk of commercial paper, lower its yield, and reduce the yield differential. The data for this variable were downloaded from Thomson Reuters' proprietary statistical database Datastream. |
| VIX | This variable represents the market expectations of volatility over the next 30-day period and is calculated by the Chicago Board Options Exchange using Standard & Poor's 500 stock index option bid/ask quotes. The variable is intended to control for volatility and uncertainty in financial markets. We expect the coefficient to be positive because increased financial market uncertainty should cause investors to move from private-sector securities into Treasury securities and reduce Treasury yields relative to other securities. The data for this variable were downloaded from proprietary data provider IHS Global Insight. |
| LOG(CPISSUE) | This is the natural log of weekly AA commercial paper issues with a maturity greater than 80 days and is intended to control for the liquidity of commercial paper. Weekly data for this variable were downloaded from the Board of Governors of the Federal Reserve System Web site and then back-filled to obtain daily values.aWe expect the variable's coefficient to be negative because an increase in liquidity should raise commercial paper prices, lower their yields, and thus decrease the yield spread. |

**Table 5. (Continued)**

| Variable name | Variable description |
|---|---|
| LOG(TBILL TRANS) | This is the natural log of weekly transactions in Treasury bills traded among primary dealers and is intended to control for the liquidity of Treasury bills. Weekly data for this variable were downloaded from the Federal Reserve Bank of New York's Web site and then back-filled to obtain daily values.bWe expect the variable's coefficient to be positive because an increase in the liquidity of Treasury bills should reduce their yield and increase the yield spread. |
| CPFFSHARE | This variable is the volume of commercial paper held by Federal Reserve through its Commercial Paper Funding Facility (CPFF) as a percentage of total commercial paper outstanding. The variable is intended tocontrol for temporary increases in liquidity from CPFF purchases. The CPFF was initiated in October 2008 to enhance the liquidity of commercial paper during the financial crisis. Because this facility did not exist during previous debt limit events, it is included only in the 2009–2010 debt limit regression. Weekly data forthis variable were downloaded from the Board of Governors of the Federal Reserve System Web site and then back-filled to obtain daily values.CWe expect the variable's coefficient to be negative because increases in liquidity should raise commercial paper prices and reduce yields, thus decreasing the yield spread. |

Source: GAO analysis.

[a] Downloaded from http://www.federalreserve.gov/DataDownload/Choose.aspx?rel=CP on May 17, 2010.

[b] Downloaded from http://www.newyorkfed.org/markets/statrel.html on May 18, 2010.

[c] Downloaded from http://www.federalreserve.gov/datadownload/Choose. aspx?rel=H41 on May 13, 2010.

The regression results based on the variables listed above are presented in table 6. Negative EVENT coefficients suggest that debt limit events reduced the spread between commercial paper and Treasury yields compared to the preevent period. Consistent with the Liu et al. (2009) study, the EVENT coefficients for the debt limit events in 2001–2002 and 2002–2003 had the expected negative sign and were statistically significant.[5] In addition, the

[5] Because these are estimates, a test of statistical significance attempts to rule out an effect purely attributable to chance. Our criterion for statistical significance is that there is less than a 10 percent probability of rejecting the null hypothesis that the coefficient is zero when the null hypothesis is true.

coefficient of the EVENT variable had the expected negative sign and was statistically significant for the most recent debt limit event in 2009–2010.

**Table 6. Regression Results for Debt Limit Event Periods from Fiscal Year 2002 to 2010**

| | | 2001–2002 | 2002–2003 | 2004–2005 | 2005–2006 | 2009–2010 |
|---|---|---|---|---|---|---|
| | Expected sign | Event 1 coefficients | Event 2 coefficients | Event 3 coefficients | Event 4 coefficients | Event 5 coefficients |
| CONSTANT | n.a. | -0.540 | 0.246 | 1.395 | -0.595 | -0.642 |
| EVENT | – | -0.011 | -0.038 | 0.025 | -0.006 | -0.040 |
| POST | –/+ | -0.011 | -0.041 | 0.034 | 0.034 | -0.030 |
| SPRET | – | -0.268 | -0.433 | -1.092 | 0.579 | 0.083 |
| VIX | + | 0.000 | -0.002 | -0.008 | 0.005 | 0.005 |
| LOG (CPISSUE) | – | 0.014 | -0.001 | 0.006 | -0.010 | 0.007 |
| LOG(TBILLT RANS) | + | 0.052 | -0.004 | -0.107 | 0.084 | 0.060 |
| CPFFSHARE | – | n.a. | n.a. | n.a. | n.a. | -0.515 |
| Number of variables with correct sign and are statistically significant | | 3 | 3 | 2 | 3 | 4 |
| Adjusted R-squared | | 0.102 | 0.241 | 0.228 | 0.029 | 0.187 |

Source: GAO analysis.

Note: The bolded coefficients have the correct signs while the cells highlighted in gray are the estimated coefficients that are statistically significant at least at the 10 percent level.

n.a.= not applicable.

We explored a variety of alternative specifications to see whether our model could be improved but found that no specification proved particularly robust across all the events studied. On the basis of discussions with Treasury staff and market experts, we added, replaced, and removed variables and defined the event period differently. For example, we explored several alternative controls for credit risk, including the spread between London interbank offer rate (LIBOR) and the Overnight Indexed Swap that measures risk and liquidity in the money market, and the spread between Baa corporate bond yields and 10-year Treasury note yields. We also redefined the event period to begin when Treasury took its first extraordinary actions or, in the case of 2009–2010, reduced the amount in the Supplementary Financing Program (SFP). None of the alternative variables or specifications produced statistically significant results. Using the Liu et al. (2009) specifications did not result in statistically significant results for the most recent event in 2009–2010.

## Effect of Debt Limit on Borrowing Costs

One the basis of our analysis, we estimate that Treasury paid $78 million in additional interest costs for newly issued 3-month securities issued during the 2009–2010 debt limit event period. We arrived at this estimate by translating the coefficient of the EVENT in 2009–2010 (-.040) to basis points (4) and multiplying by the amount of 3-month Treasury bills issued during the event period. We selected 3-month bills for our analysis because it is a commonly used benchmark in economic indicators such as the TED spread—a key indicator of credit risk.[6] We did not estimate the effects of the debt limit on other Treasury securities with longer terms to maturity in part because of a lack of reliable data on yields for private-sector fixed-income assets with maturity dates comparable to medium-term Treasury securities such as a 2-year note. Therefore, we do not know whether the same 4-basis-point premium would apply to other Treasury securities with longer or shorter terms to maturity issued during the debt limit event period. Nippani et al. (2001) found that the effect of the debate over the debt limit in 1995–1996 was greater on 3-month Treasury bills than on 6-month Treasury bills, indicating the investors may have believed that debate over the debt limit would be resolved over time and that longer-dated securities would therefore be less affected. However, even a smaller premium when applied to the large amount of Treasury securities offered by Treasury would result in a notable increase in borrowing costs. For instance, for each additional basis point paid on bills issued during the 2009–2010 debt limit event period, Treasury's borrowing cost would increase by roughly $92 million.

6 The TED spread is the difference between the 3-month LIBOR rate and 3-month Treasury yield.

## Limitations of the Analysis

There are a number of limitations to using a multivariate regression to measure changes in Treasury's borrowing costs. First, the results of our analysis explain only a small portion of the variation in the yield spread, as indicated by the relatively low R-squared statistics. Any equation attempting to explain the yield spread would have limited explanatory power given inherent randomness in daily time series data such as Treasury bill and commercial paper yields. Furthermore, the estimates are subject to omitted variable bias. Second, there was substantial variation in the sign, size, and significance of the estimated coefficients across debt limit events. However, the EVENT variable's coefficient, which is the central focus of our analysis, had the expected negative sign in four of the five debt limit periods included in our analysis and was significant in three of these periods. We discussed these and other limitations with Treasury officials, staff at the Federal Reserve Bank of New York, and other market experts such as primary dealers and incorporated their suggestions and feedback when appropriate. Despite these limitations, the estimates do suggest that a debt limit event may result in a premium.

## End Notes

[1] A very small amount of total federal debt is not subject to the debt limit. This amount is primarily comprised of unamortized discounts on Treasury bills and Zero Coupon Treasury bonds; debt securities issued by agencies other than Treasury, such as the Tennessee Valley Authority; and debt securities issued by the Federal Financing Bank. As of September 30, 2010, 99.5 percent of federal debt was subject to the debt limit.

[2] Budget resolutions are concurrent resolutions, which are not presented to the President for his signature and do not become law. Therefore, debt limit increases must be passed as part of separate legislation such as a bill or joint resolution.

[3] This was House Rule XXVIII in the 111th Congress but was not included in the House Rules for the 112th Congress.

[4] Pub. L. No. 111-5. The other acts were the Housing and Economic Recovery Act of 2008 (Pub. L. No. 110-289) and the Emergency Economic Stabilization Act of 2008 (Pub. L. No. 110-343).

[5] We have issued a number of prior reports on Treasury's efforts to achieve this goal including more recently *Debt Management: Treasury Was Able to Fund Economic Stabilization and Recovery Expenditures in a Short Period of Time, but Debt Management Challenges Remain*, GAO-10-498 (Washington, D.C.: May 18, 2010), *Debt Management: Treasury Inflation Protected Securities Should Play a Heightened Role in Addressing Debt Management Challenges*, GAO-09-932 (Washington, D.C.: Sept. 29, 2009), and *Debt*

*Management: Treasury Has Refined Its Use of Cash Management Bills but Should Explore Options That May Reduce Cost Further*, GAO-06-269 (Washington, D.C.: Mar. 30, 2006).

[6] See http://www.gao.gov/special.pubs/longterm/debt/, which updates information in *Federal Debt: Answers to Frequently Asked Questions: An Update,* GAO-04-485SP (Washington, D.C.: Aug. 12, 2004).

[7] Treasury generally uses CM bills to finance intramonth funding gaps due to timing differences of large cash inflows and outflows but has also used them in recent years to raise funds for the Supplementary Financing Program—a temporary program begun in 2008 to assist the Federal Reserve with its monetary policy.

[8] For information on the costs associated with issuing CM bills, see GAO-06-269 and GAO-10-498.

[9] Pub. L. No. 104-103 (Feb. 8, 1996).

[10] For additional information on the costs associated with past transactions, see GAO, *Debt Ceiling: Analysis of Actions Taken during the 2003 Debt Issuance Suspension Period*, GAO-04-526 (Washington, D.C.: May 20, 2004).

[11] Treasury also called back compensating balances after a cancellation of a 4-week bill auction the week of September 11, 2001, to help meet its obligations on time.

[12] Interest payments on debt held in government accounts are credited to government accounts and do not require additional borrowing from the public, but the investment of these interest payments is subject to the debt limit.

[13] The increase in nonmarketable debt on December 31, 2009, includes roughly $18 billion in interest payments on debt held by the CSRDF trust fund that Treasury could choose to suspend during a DISP.

[14] Cash held in the Treasury's Supplementary Financing Program account is excluded because it has not been used to finance federal expenditures.

[15] The amount of disinvestment of securities held by CSRDF is determined based on the length of the declared DISP, which affects the total amount of the available extraordinary actions.

[16] GAO-06-269.

[17] Our methodology was based on a prior academic study: Pu Liu, Yingying Shao, and Timothy J. Yeager, "Did the repeated debt ceiling controversies embed default risk in U.S. Treasury securities?" *Journal of Banking & Finance*, vol. 33 (2009): 1464-1471. The regression specification we used for the recent debt limit was different from the Liu et al. regression specification because the financial markets were operating in unique economic conditions (e.g., the Federal Reserve began purchasing commercial paper in 2008 to enhance the liquidity of the commercial paper market). We also reviewed a similar study: Srinivas Nippani, Pu Liu, and Craig T. Schulman, "Are Treasury Securities Free of Default?" *Journal of Financial and Quantitative Analysis*, vol. 36, no. 2 (2001): 251-265. This study also found that the market charged a premium on Treasury securities issued during the debt limit debate in 1995-1996. See app. II for more information.

[18] For the purposes of this study, a debt limit event period begins when Treasury first warns of the need to raise the debt limit and ends when legislation to raise the limit is passed. For the first four debt limit events, we use the same dates used by Liu et al. (2009). For the fifth debt limit event in 2009–2010, the event period began when Treasury notified Congress that the debt limit needed to be raised and ended when legislation increasing the debt limit was signed into law.

[19] This is consistent with the Liu et al. (2009). The authors of the study hypothesized that during these latter two debt limit events, investors may have assumed based on past experience that members of Congress would resolve their differences before there were any serious

disruptions in the Treasury market and therefore did not charge a premium on securities issued near the debt limit.

[20] The 95 percent confidence interval of the premium estimate ranges from 1.0 to 7.1 basis points.

[21] Standard & Poor's, *The U.S. Debt Ceiling: As Headroom Shrinks, It's Time to Raise the Room Beams* (Oct. 9, 2009).

[22] Moody's, *U.S. Statutory Debt Limit to be Raised; Longer-Term Fiscal Strategy the Real Question* (September 2009).

[23] Automatic stabilizers are provisions built into the structure of the federal budget that alter tax or spending levels based on economic fluctuations without any explicit government action.

[24] Under 31 U.S.C. § 1106, the President is required to submit an update of the federal budget, often referred to as a mid-session review, before July 16 of each year.

[25] Congress reached agreement on budget procedures in the Balanced Budget and Emergency Deficit Control Act of 1985 (Pub. L. No. 99-177), Balanced Budget and Emergency Deficit Control Reaffirmation Act of 1987 (Pub. L. No. 100-119), the Budget Enforcement Act of 1990 (Pub. L. No. 101-508), the extended budget process provisions of the Budget Enforcement Act of 1990 (Pub. L. No. 103-66), and the Budget Enforcement Act of 1997 (Pub. L. No. 105-33).

[26] PAYGO is a procedure requiring that the aggregate effect of increases in mandatory spending or reductions in revenue generally be offset (Pub. L. No. 111-139).

[27] These are the National Commission on Fiscal Responsibility and Reform, *The Moment of Truth: Report of the National Commission on Fiscal Responsibility and Reform* (Washington, D.C.: December 2010); Bipartisan Policy Center, *Restoring America's Future: Reviving the Economy, Cutting Spending and Debt, and Creating a Simple Pro-Growth Tax System* (Washington, D.C.: November 2010); National Research Council and National Academy of Public Administration, *Choosing the Nation's Fiscal Future* (Washington, D.C.: 2010); and Peterson-Pew Commission on Budget Reform, *Red Ink Rising: A Call to Action to Stem Mounting Federal Debt* (Washington, D.C.: December 2009).

[28] The American Recovery and Reinvestment Act of 2009 (Pub. L. No. 111-5), the Housing and Economic Recovery Act of 2008 (Pub. L. No. 110-289) and the Emergency Economic Stabilization Act of 2008 (Pub. L. No. 110-343).

In: Debt Limit Management... ISBN: 978-1-61324-418-0
Editors: J. D. Antonellis, N. P. Barone 

*Chapter 4*

# DEBT MANAGEMENT: TREASURY INFLATION PROTECTED SECURITIES SHOULD PLAY A HEIGHTENED ROLE IN ADDRESSING DEBT MANAGEMENT CHALLENGES*

***United States Government Accountability Office***

## WHY GAO DID THIS STUDY

The 2008 financial market crisis and the economic recession led to a rapid and substantial increase in federal debt. This report, part of a line of work on debt management, was conducted under the Comptroller General's authority. It describes current debt management challenges and examines the role of a program that could benefit Treasury—Treasury Inflation Protected Securities (TIPS). GAO analyzed market data and interviewed experts as well as the two largest holders of Treasury securities in each of six sectors.

* This is an edited, reformatted and augmented version of the United States Government Accountability Office's publication, dated September 2009.

## WHAT GAO RECOMMENDS

GAO recommends that, in the context of projected sustained increases in federal debt, the Secretary of the Treasury take steps to increase TIPS liquidity and reduce their cost to Treasury: increase issuance, issue longer-dated maturities, and conduct more frequent auctions. Also, the Secretary should continually review the appropriate composition of the TIPS program and consider: the impact of Treasury's public statements and TIPS issuance on TIPS liquidity, how different analytical perspectives are valuable for evaluating cost, how TIPS can diversify Treasury's investor base, and how TIPS impact the cost of nominal securities.

Treasury took note of our findings, conclusions, and recommendations and said they were consistent with their commitment to increasing TIPS issuance.

## WHAT GAO FOUND

In January 1997, Treasury introduced an inflation-indexed security—TIPS. Treasury's stated objectives were to both raise the national savings rate and to reduce the federal government's cost of borrowing. TIPS offer inflation protection to investors who are willing to pay a premium for this protection in the form of a lower interest rate. In a functioning TIPS market, the difference between the interest rate on nominal Treasury securities and the interest rate on TIPS is expected to be approximately equal to the expected inflation rate.

Federal government actions in response to both the financial market crisis and the economic recession have added significantly to Treasury's borrowing needs. Since the onset of the recession in December 2007, Treasury has borrowed more than $2.3 trillion, largely by issuing short-term nominal debt, which significantly changed the composition of Treasury's debt portfolio. The challenges presented by increasing debt and the change in its composition take place in the context of the medium and longer term fiscal outlook and will not recede with the return of financial market stability and economic growth. The Congressional Budget Office (CBO) projects that, absent changes in current policy, debt held by the public will double in 5 years (from 2008 to 2013) and almost triple in 11 years (from 2008 to 2019)—reaching 82 percent of GDP. In order to meet these challenges Treasury needs to diversify its funding sources and lengthen the term-to-maturity of its debt portfolio. TIPS can contribute to this effort.

Treasury's TIPS program has had varying degrees of liquidity (the ease with which investors can trade the security) since its inception. The major institutional investors that GAO interviewed perceived Treasury's commitment to the TIPS program as having wavered in recent years, decreasing the liquidity of TIPS in the market. Investors demand a premium for holding less-liquid TIPS, which increases Treasury's borrowing costs.

TIPS offer benefits to Treasury and measuring the cost against which to weigh these benefits requires both forward-looking and after-the-fact analysis. A more robust TIPS program could benefit Treasury by diversifying and expanding its funding sources and reducing the cost of nominal securities. Governments are well suited to bear inflation risk because periods of inflation are often associated with increased revenues. TIPS auctions also help provide a measure of market inflation expectations.

On July 1, 2009, GAO briefed Treasury's Office of Debt Management on the findings from our analysis and interviews with major institutional investors. Treasury later posed questions about ways to improve the TIPS program to the Primary Dealers and the Treasury Borrowing Advisory Committee (TBAC). At the August 2009 TBAC meeting, members discussed TIPS. Following the meeting, Treasury's Deputy Assistant Secretary for Federal Finance reaffirmed Treasury's commitment to TIPS and announced plans to gradually increase issuance of TIPS.

## LIST OF ABBREVIATIONS

| | |
|---|---|
| CBO | Congressional Budget Office |
| CPI-U | Consumer Price Index for All Urban Consumers |
| GDP | gross domestic product |
| ODM | Office of Debt Management |
| OMB | Office of Management and Budget |
| SIFMA | Securities Industry and Financial Markets Association |
| TARP | Troubled Asset Relief Program |
| TBAC | Treasury Borrowing Advisory Committee |
| TIPS | Treasury Inflation Protected Securities September 29, 2009 |

The Honorable Timothy F. Geithner

Secretary of the Treasury

Dear Mr. Secretary:

Between December 2007 and the end of June 2009, the Department of the Treasury borrowed more than $2.3 trillion to finance federal government actions related to both the financial market crisis and the economic recession in addition to regular government financing needs. This rapid and substantial increase in federal debt takes place in the context of the medium- and long-term fiscal outlook that will present Treasury with continued financing challenges long after the return of financial stability and economic growth. GAO has begun a line of work related to Treasury's management of its growing debt portfolio. As part of this ongoing work, we will continue to provide updates and make recommendations as appropriate.

In this first report, conducted under the Comptroller General's authority, we describe Treasury's borrowing challenges and analyze one Treasury program that has the potential to provide benefits to both Treasury and investors—Treasury Inflation Protected Securities (TIPS). We address the following questions:

- What are the debt management challenges associated with planning for future borrowing needs given the long-term fiscal outlook and Treasury's increased borrowing due to economic and financial sector stress?
- What role, if any, should TIPS play in Treasury's borrowing program?

## BACKGROUND

Congress has assigned to Treasury the responsibility of borrowing the funds necessary to finance the gap between cash-in and cash-out, subject to a statutory limit. Treasury's primary debt management goal is to finance the government's borrowing needs at the lowest cost over time. Issuing debt predictably through regularly scheduled auctions lowers borrowing costs because investors and dealers value liquidity and certainty of supply. Treasury responds to increases in borrowing needs in a traditional manner, by first increasing the issuance size of existing securities; then, increasing the frequency of issuances; and finally, introducing new securities to its auction calendar as necessary.

Treasury normally auctions nominal marketable securities that range in maturity from 4 weeks to 30 years and sells them at auction on a pre-announced schedule. Treasury also issues cash management bills that are not part of the regular schedule to meet immediate cash needs. Treasury securities are widely viewed as the premium risk-free asset and are actively used by investors, traders, and foreign central banks for hedging, liquidity, and reserve purposes. The outstanding mix of U.S. Treasury securities can have a significant influence on the federal government's interest payments. Longer term securities typically carry higher interest rates (which translate to increased cost to the government), primarily due to concerns about future inflation. However, these longer term securities offer the government the certainty of fixing the interest payments over a longer period and reduce the amount of debt that Treasury needs to refinance in the short term. In contrast, shorter term securities generally carry lower interest rates but add volatility to the government's interest costs and require Treasury to conduct more frequent auctions to refinance maturing debt.

During the 1980s and 1990s, a number of countries introduced inflation-indexed securities to their debt offerings, including the United Kingdom, France, and the United States.[1] In January 1997, Treasury introduced its own inflation-indexed securities, TIPS, as part of its debt program. At the time, Treasury's stated objectives for introducing TIPS were both to raise the national savings rate and to reduce the federal government's cost of borrowing. TIPS offer inflation protection to investors who are willing to pay a premium for this protection in the form of a lower interest rate. In a functioning TIPS market, the difference between the interest rate on nominal Treasury securities and the interest rate on TIPS should approximately equal the expected inflation rate. Treasury currently issues 5-, 10-, and 20-year TIPS. In the past, Treasury issued 30-year TIPS, but discontinued them in 2001. See appendix I for additional details on the structure of TIPS.

## SCOPE AND METHODOLOGY

To identify the debt management challenges associated with Treasury's increased borrowing, we analyzed the scale, timing, term to maturity, and composition of Treasury's borrowing since the start of the economic recession, using data and information obtained from the Department of the Treasury and the Federal Reserve. We also interviewed market experts, Treasury, and Federal Reserve staff and officials.

To examine what role TIPS should play in Treasury's debt portfolio and the potential for the TIPS program to help address Treasury's debt management challenges, we conducted literature reviews on the costs and benefits of inflation-indexed securities and examined research by Federal Reserve economists, market experts, academic sources, and the Department of the Treasury, including an internal review of the TIPS program done by the Office of Debt Management (ODM). We also conducted 12 structured interviews in June 2009 with the two largest holders of Treasury securities in each of the following sectors: mutual funds; commercial banks; life insurance companies; property and casualty insurance companies; state and local pension funds; and private pension funds. The major institutional investors we interviewed held at least $351 billion in Treasury securities. Of their Treasury holdings, $99.4 billion were TIPS, which was 19 percent of total outstanding TIPS as of March 31, 2009. These interviews covered the institution's holdings of Treasury securities, demand for TIPS, changes that could be made to the TIPS program, perceived risks to investors in Treasury markets, and Treasury's sources for information on demand for Treasury securities. On July 1, 2009, we briefed Treasury's ODM on the findings from the structured interviews, which are discussed and expanded upon in this report.[2]

Where possible and appropriate, we corroborated the results of our data analyses and interviews with other sources. On the basis of our assessment we believe that the data are reliable for the purposes of our review. We conducted our review from June 2009 through August 2009 in accordance with generally accepted government auditing standards. Those standards require that we plan and perform the audit to obtain sufficient, appropriate evidence to provide a reasonable basis for our findings and conclusions based on our audit objectives. We believe that the evidence obtained provides a reasonable basis for our findings and conclusions based on our audit objectives.

## SIZE AND COMPOSITION OF TREASURY'S DEBT PROFILE HAS CHANGED SUBSTANTIALLY

Treasury faces two near-term challenges in managing the growing government debt: the rise in total outstanding debt and the shortening of the average maturity of the debt profile.[3] Treasury's total outstanding debt increased by $2.3 trillion (25 percent increase in federal debt) since the onset of the economic recession in December 2007.[4] In actions Treasury described as in accordance with normal operating procedures, Treasury increased short-term borrowing to address its massive and immediate borrowing needs. As a result, the average maturity of Treasury's debt decreased as the percentage of marketable debt maturing within 1 year increased from 35.6 percent to 41.1 percent between September 2007 and June 2009. At the end of June 2009, Treasury's outstanding marketable securities stood at $6.6 trillion, an increase of almost $2.1 trillion from December 2007.[5] The largest increase in outstanding marketable Treasury securities was in short-term debt. Treasury bill and cash management bill issuance increased by a combined $1 trillion between December 2007 and June 2009.[6] The amount of Treasury notes issued also increased significantly over this period, adding $929.3 billion to the amount of notes outstanding. Almost half of the increase was comprised of shorter-term notes (with 2-year and 5-year maturities). The monthly issuance of 2-year notes alone has almost doubled in the last 2 years. Figure 1 shows the relative size of the increases in different categories of securities. The smallest increase was in TIPS which increased by $60.6 billion.

Treasury has raised significant amounts of cash since the onset of the economic recession in December 2007 largely by adhering to its regular and predictable debt issuance schedule, which is meant to ensure the lowest borrowing costs over time. However, Treasury has also turned to issuing cash management bills, which are announced shortly before auction to fulfill Treasury's immediate cash needs. After the financial market crisis hit in fall of 2008, Treasury raised an unprecedented $1.1 trillion in under 18 weeks largely by issuing cash management bills. Treasury was able to finance such an amount due in part to outsized demand among global investors for a safe and liquid financial instrument in the midst of the contraction in global economic activity.

As shown in figure 2, 78 percent (or about $5.1 trillion) of the outstanding marketable Treasuries mature by 2015 and will need to be rolled over (or refinanced)—potentially at higher interest rates. Because short-term rates have been reduced sharply by the decision of the Federal Reserve to set its federal funds target near zero, Treasury's borrowing costs decreased even though debt levels increased. (See figure 3.) However, projections from both the Congressional Budget Office (CBO) and Office of Management and Budget (OMB) assume higher interest rates and higher interest payments. CBO's analysis of the President's Budgetary Proposals for Fiscal Year 2010 assumed that interest rates on 91-day Treasury bills would increase from 0.3 percent in 2009 to 4.7 percent in 2015 and that interest on 10-year Treasury notes would increase from 2.9 percent to 5.4 percent over the same period. CBO's analysis of the President's Budgetary Proposals for Fiscal Year 2010 shows—absent changes in policy—interest payments on federal debt more than tripling—to almost $800 billion—by 2019.[7] (See figure 3.)

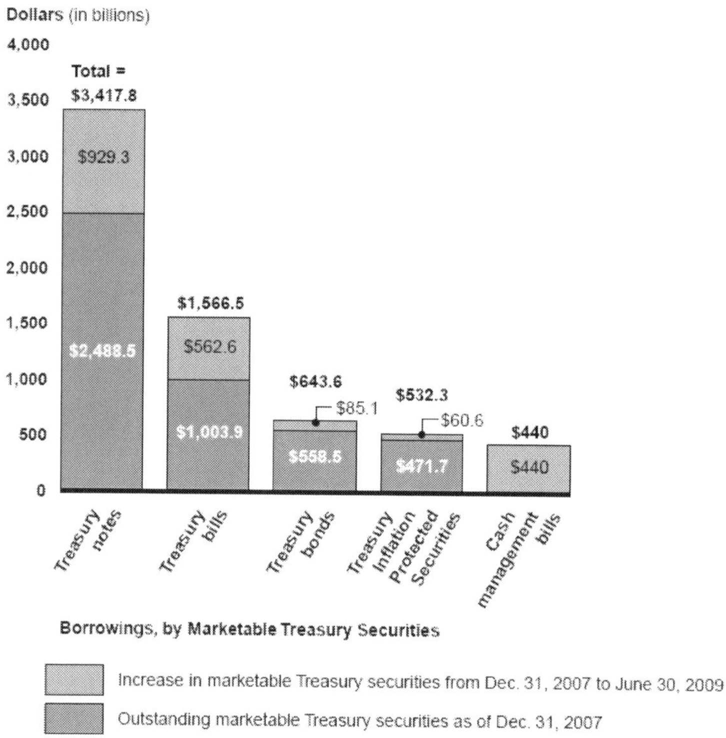


Source: GAO analysis of Treasury monthly statement of public debt data.

Note: Does not include $11.9 billion in marketable securities outstanding for the Federal Financing Bank. Treasury bills and cash management bills are short-term securities that mature in 1 year or less from their issue date. Treasury notes mature in more than 1 year, but not more than 10 years from their issue date. Treasury bonds mature in more than 10 years from their issue date. Treasury bills, notes, and bonds are nominal securities, meaning they are not adjusted for inflation. TIPS are adjusted for inflation and have maturities of 5, 10, or 20 years.

Figure 1. Changes in Outstanding Marketable Treasury Securities from December 31, 2007, to June 30, 2009 (Total Outstanding as of June 30, 2009—$6.6 trillion).

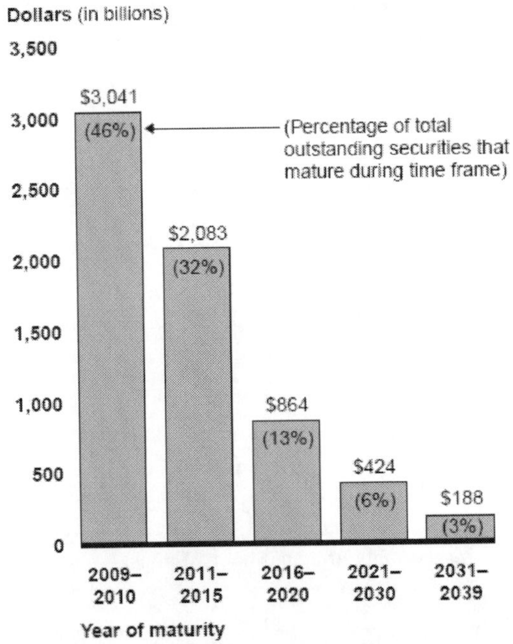


Source: GAO analysis of Treasury monthly statement of public debt data.

Note: Does not include $11.9 billion in marketable securities outstanding for the Federal Financing Bank, $43 million in matured notes, and $45 million in matured bonds.

Figure 2. Marketable Securities by Year of Maturity, as of June 30, 2009 (Total Outstanding—$6.6 trillion).

Treasury's Director of ODM and the ODM staff whom we interviewed view the current maturity profile as reasonable given economic conditions and the massive increase in borrowing that was necessary in a compressed time period. They underscored the importance of making any changes to the current debt portfolio in a gradual manner to ensure that there will be enough demand at a reasonable price and told us that they plan to gradually transition the portfolio into longer term debt.[8] They also told us that, given the need to be flexible operationally, Treasury's debt management horizon is shorter than the horizon used by CBO and OMB in budget projections and that they are confident about their ability to finance the projected budget deficits for 2010 and 2011.

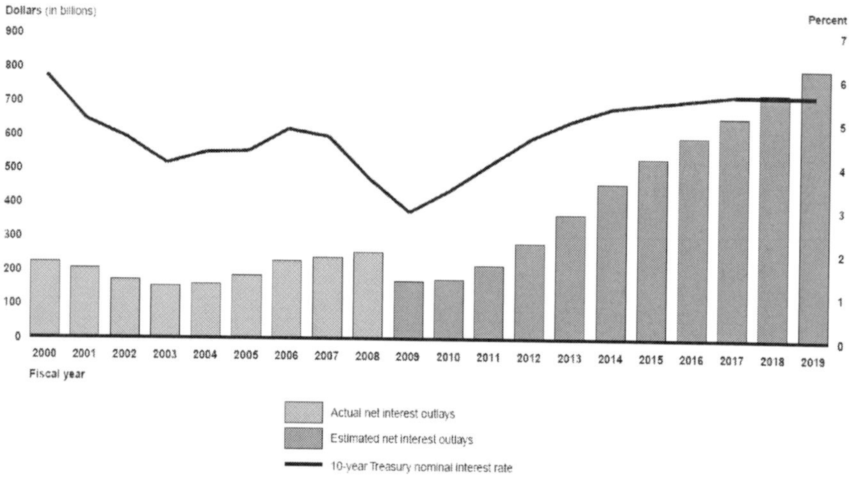


Sources: Congressional Budget Office data from their analysis of the President's budget proposal of actual and estimated net interest costs and estimated interest rates and Federal Reserve data of actual interest rates.

Note: Net interest outlays is a cash measure that is defined as interest payments on gross debt less interest received on loans and advances, and is affected by the volume of net debt on issue and by interest rates.

Figure 3. Net Interest Costs and 10-Year Treasury Rates.

## Fiscal Outlook Will Present Continued Debt Management Challenges

As noted, the federal government's policy response to the financial market crisis and the economic recession created a significant increase in both debt and debt management challenges. These will not recede when stability returns to financial markets and economic growth resumes. CBO projects that, absent changes in current policy, the debt held by the public will double in 5 years (from 2008 to 2013) and almost triple in 11 years (from 2008 to 2019). (See figure 4.) CBO projects that debt held by the public will increase from 41 percent of gross domestic product (GDP) in fiscal year 2008 to 71 percent by the end of fiscal year 2013.

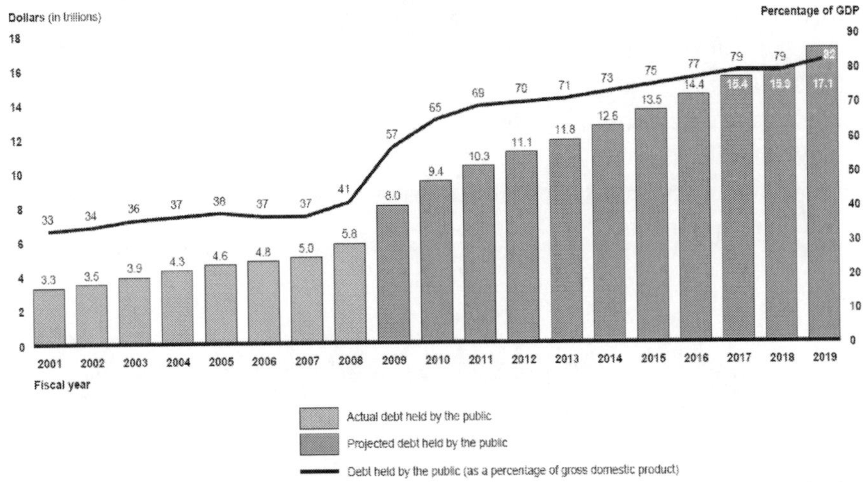


Source: Congressional Budget Office data from their analysis of the President's budget proposal.

Figure 4. Debt Held by the Public and Percentage of GDP, 2001 through 2019.

The actions that Treasury has taken to increase borrowing in response to the economic recession and financial market crisis take place within the context of the already serious longer term fiscal condition of the federal government. While the administration and Congress have been understandably focused on addressing problems with financial markets and responding to the economic recession, the government will need to apply the same level of intensity to the nation's long-term fiscal challenge. Both our long-term simulations and CBO's show growing deficits and debt, underscoring that the long-term fiscal outlook is unsustainable. Under our alternative simulation, by 2025 debt held by the public would exceed the historical high of 109 percent of GDP, reached in the aftermath of World War II.[9] (See figure 5.)

The deterioration in the short-term and long-term budget outlooks, combined with expenditures associated with the Troubled Asset Relief Program (TARP) and Recovery Act spending, will likely continue to stress the existing auction schedule. Treasury has already begun to respond by adjusting the auction schedule so that they can conduct more auctions of increasingly larger amounts, while simultaneously minimizing borrowing costs over the long term.

According to the major institutional investors that we interviewed, the best days of the week for Treasury to conduct auctions are Tuesday, Wednesday, and Thursday. However, Treasury is facing an increasingly crowded borrowing schedule, often with multiple auctions in a single day. For example, during the week of July 27, 2009, Treasury held eight auctions, issuing close to $272 billion in securities in one week and holding multiple auctions on two of those days. In addition, Treasury has been forced to hold and plan auctions on days that it has tried to avoid in the past, such as days of major Federal Reserve announcements. Holding auctions on these days increases uncertainty for auction participants.

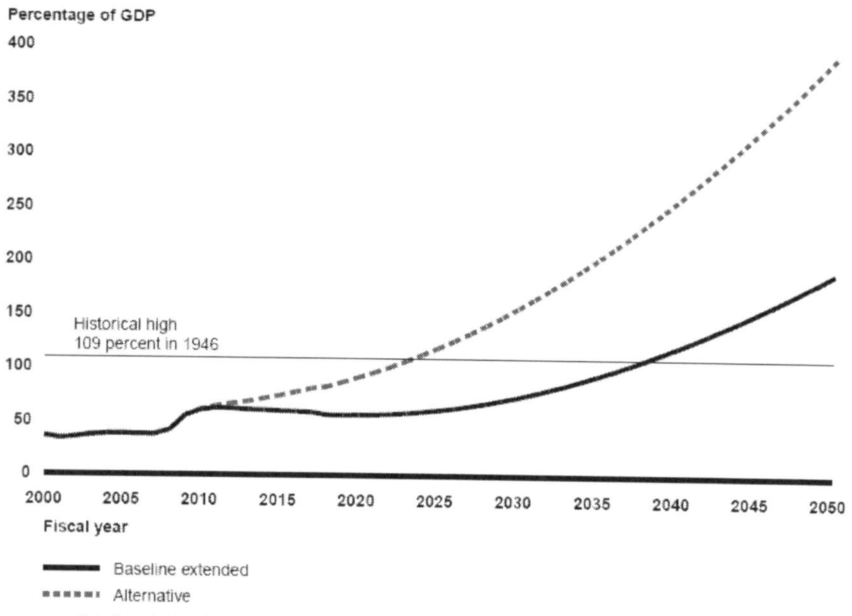


Source: GAO's March 2009 analysis based on the Trustees' assumptions for Social Security and Medicare. (See GAO, *The Nation's Long-Term Fiscal Outlook March 2009 Update*, GAO-09-405SP (Washington, D.C.: April 30, 2009).

Figure 5. Debt Held by the Public as a Share of GDP under Two Different Fiscal Policy Simulations.

Market experts believe that the large amount of the debt that must be rolled over in the next few years is cause for concern and agree with Treasury that it needs to increase the average maturity of its debt portfolio and diversify its funding sources. Large and growing borrowing needs put a premium on better understanding current and future demand for Treasury securities. Two securities that Treasury can currently use to reduce the amount of securities that are rolling over in the next 10 years are 30-year nominal bonds and 20-year TIPS.[10] Treasury has already increased the frequency of the issuance of

30-year bonds; first it reopened the 30-year bond in February 2009 and then added a second reopening in May 2009, effectively issuing the 30-year bond on a monthly basis. Treasury should continue to consider options to lengthen its maturity profile to mitigate the risks mentioned above. Longer-dated TIPS offer one option. The 30-year TIPS was discontinued along with the 30-year nominal bond in October 2001, but only the 30-year nominal bond was reintroduced. The 20-year TIPS, is currently issued only twice a year, but its record as a low-cost funding source has been mixed in part due to a lack of liquidity as explained in the next section.

## TREASURY'S TIPS PROGRAM HAS HAD VARYING DEGREES OF LIQUIDITY SINCE INCEPTION AND MAJOR INSTITUTIONAL INVESTORS HAVE EXPRESSED CONCERN ABOUT TREASURY'S COMMITMENT TO THE PROGRAM

Treasury's TIPS program has had varying degrees of liquidity since its inception in 1997. Liquidity is a measure of the ease with which investors can trade a security. Liquidity is important to Treasury because liquid securities can be auctioned at lower rates, and thus cost Treasury less money.

The difference between the breakeven inflation rate—the interest rate on a nominal security minus the interest rate on a comparable-maturity TIPS— and a measure of expected inflation can be used to evaluate the ex-ante cost of nominal securities relative to TIPS.[11] When this difference is positive, nominal securities cost more than TIPS; when it is negative, TIPS cost more than nominal securities; and when the difference is zero, the cost is approximately equivalent. Two primary factors affect this difference. The first is the illiquidity premium associated with TIPS, which raises the interest rate on TIPS relative to nominal securities. The second is the inflation risk premium, which is the insurance value that investors attach to TIPS' protection against inflation. The inflation risk premium reduces the interest rate on TIPS relative to the rate on nominal securities. To the degree that the inflation risk premium and illiquidity premium are roughly equal, nominal Treasury securities and TIPS of the same maturity would cost about the same, on an ex-ante (or before the fact) basis. For a more detailed discussion on calculating the cost of TIPS compared to nominal securities see appendix II.

In 1997, when the TIPS program was launched, the initial auctions were well-received by investors, with robust bid-to-cover ratios.[12] As seen in figure

6, the average 10-year breakeven rate minus expected inflation in 1997 was the largest seen to date on the 10-year TIPS. Thereafter, from 1998 until about 2004, TIPS liquidity remained relatively poor and the gross amount issued by Treasury decreased from 1998 to 2000.

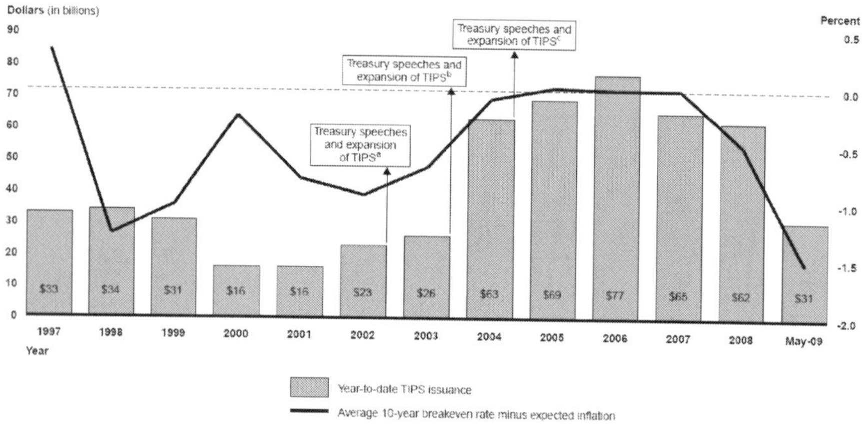


Source: GAO analysis of Treasury data on TIPS issuances and Federal Reserve Bank of Philadelphia's Survey of Professional Forecasters Inflation Expectations.

[a] Treasury official announcement on expansion of TIPS on May 1, 2002. Treasury speech bolstering TIPS program on June 3, 2002, October 17, 2002, November 8, 2002, and December 5, 2002.

[b] Treasury official announcement on expansion of TIPS on April 30, 2003. Treasury speech bolstering TIPS program on May 20, 2003 and June 26, 2003.

[c] Treasury official announcement on expansion of TIPS on May 4, 2004. Treasury speech bolstering TIPS program on April 22, 2004, June 16, 2004, and July 8, 2004.

Figure 6. Treasury's Statements of Support for TIPS, Gross TIPS Issuance, and the TIPS Program's Relative Costs.

Starting in 2002, Treasury sought input from market participants on how to improve the TIPS program and made a number of changes to the program. Specifically, Treasury increased the amount issued at auction and increased the frequency and range of TIPS offerings. In addition, Treasury made a number of speeches and official statements to reaffirm its commitment to the program and to indicate its dedication to improving TIPS liquidity. Some of the major institutional investors we interviewed observed that these efforts improved investor confidence in the program and ultimately improved the liquidity of TIPS. As seen in figure 6, from 2004 to 2007, the difference between the average 10-year breakeven rate and inflation expectations was positive or near zero, meaning the TIPS illiquidity premium was approximately equal to the inflation risk premium of nominal securities and indicating that TIPS liquidity improved over that period.

More recently, from 2006 to 2008, Treasury reduced the gross amount of TIPS issuance by 19 percent. The major institutional investors that we interviewed also perceived that during this time, Treasury's commitment to the TIPS program began to wane, communicating uncertainty about the program's future. These investors believed that the uncertainty surrounding TIPS hurt TIPS liquidity in the secondary market.

In the period following the 2008 financial market crisis, TIPS liquidity further deteriorated as demand for the more liquid nominal Treasury securities soared. The illiquidity premium, or the extra compensation that Treasury has to pay investors to hold TIPS, may have increased during the financial crisis due to the increased difficulty of selling holdings of TIPS in the secondary market during that time. Major institutional investors whom we interviewed reported uncertainty about Treasury's commitment to the TIPS program and suggested increased issuance and positive signaling to improve the liquidity of TIPS, thereby reducing the cost of the program to Treasury.

## Major Institutional Investors Report Uncertainty about Treasury's Commitment to TIPS and Suggest Increased Issuance and Positive Signaling to Improve the Liquidity of TIPS

Interviews with major institutional investors revealed uncertainty about Treasury's commitment to TIPS. The investors pointed to the 19 percent decline in TIPS gross issuance amounts, along with Treasury's tepid signaling on TIPS, as fueling speculation about the future of the program.[13] (See figure 6.) As of June 2009, TIPS made up about 8 percent of total outstanding marketable Treasury securities, compared to 10 percent in September 2007 and 2008.

As we reported to Treasury, on July 1, 2009, there was agreement among the major institutional investors whom we interviewed that Treasury could improve liquidity in the TIPS market by signaling to the market its commitment to the program and by increasing issuance. Investors suggested that Treasury repeat efforts to promote the TIPS program as they did from 2002 to 2004. Investors told us that increasing the issuance amount at auction or increasing the frequency of auctions would have a similar signaling effect and the additional supply would also improve liquidity in the secondary market. Most of the investors replied that they planned to purchase TIPS in the next year; interest in the 10-year TIPS was mentioned most frequently. Some investors stated that their organizations would be more likely to participate in the TIPS market if the supply of securities was greater and auctions were conducted more frequently. Some investors reported wanting to make larger TIPS purchases than was possible in the secondary market and also that the long wait between TIPS auctions sometimes did not align with their investment needs. Currently, there is a 6-month wait between auctions for 5-year and 20-year TIPS and a 3-month wait between auctions for 10-year TIPS.

At our briefing, Treasury's Director of ODM and ODM staff told us that if it were to expand the TIPS program, Treasury would face increased exposure to auction risk due to the current concentration of bidders at auction and the resulting possibility that there may not be enough bidders to cover the auctioned amount. But Treasury already has policies in place to ensure that potentially undersubscribed auctions are sufficiently covered. In addition to these policies, investors we interviewed told us that a more formalized line of communication between Treasury and end-users could enable Treasury to better gauge market demand. We are in the process of surveying investors on what actions Treasury could take to increase participation in TIPS auctions and improve communication with end-users of Treasury securities.

One indicator used to measure demand at a Treasury auction is the bid-to-cover ratio, which compares the dollars bid to the dollars accepted at a Treasury auction. If the ratio is high, it indicates strong demand for a particular Treasury security at auction. There is historical evidence that auctions in the TIPS market have bid-to-cover ratios only slightly lower than the more robust market for nominal securities. As shown in figure 7, for most of the period prior to 2009, TIPS auctions had slightly lower bidto-cover ratios than comparable nominal securities. But more recently, differences between TIPS and nominal bid-to-cover ratios have decreased. From January to July of 2009, the average bid-to-cover ratio for 5-, 10-, and 30-year nominal auctions has been 2.30. The average bid-to-cover ratio of 5-, 10-, and 20-year TIPS auctions has been 2.31 during the same period.

Treasury's current policies to ensure sufficient coverage of auctions were instituted after a 10-year nominal Treasury note auction had a relatively low bid-to-cover ratio of 1.2 in May 2003. The more recent, stronger bid-tocover ratios indicate that the market would support increased TIPS issuance. A more liquid TIPS market would benefit Treasury. At the same time, the cost to Treasury of the TIPS program going forward remains a subject of debate.

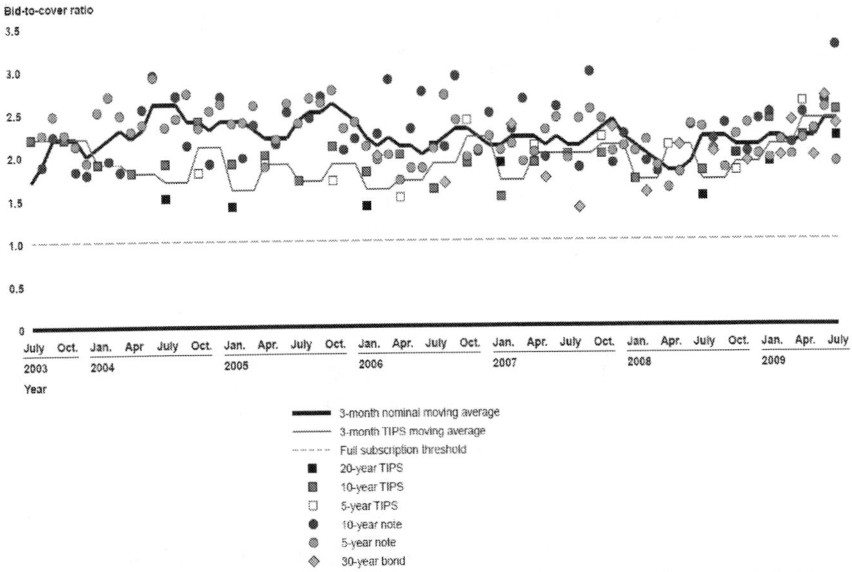


Source: GAO analysis of Treasury auction data on 5-year, 10-year, and 30-year nominal Treasury securities and 5-year, 10-year, 20-year, and 30-year TIPS.

Figure 7. Bid-to-Cover Ratios for Selected Treasury Securities, July 2003 to July 2009.

# TIPS Program Offers Benefits to Treasury, and Measuring Its Cost Requires both Forward-Looking and after-the-Fact Analysis

TIPS offer a variety of benefits to both Treasury and investors. TIPS provide Treasury the opportunity to diversify its investor base because TIPS are by design a very different product than nominal securities. In addition, TIPS may reduce the cost of nominal securities. The cost against which to weigh the benefits of TIPS, however, is unclear. While there is agreement on the higher initial cost of the TIPS program, less consensus exists on the total cost of the TIPS program to date.

## TIPS Program Could Benefit Treasury by Diversifying Its Funding Sources and Investor Base

TIPS could benefit Treasury by diversifying its funding sources and investor base. Market experts and researchers, including the Securities Industry and Financial Markets Association (SIFMA), asserted that TIPS could provide Treasury with access to new investors whose needs could complement those of investors in nominal securities.[14] In a 2004 letter to Treasury, the Bond Market Association, now part of SIFMA, stated that "the Association continues to believe that the Treasury's TIPS program is likely to ultimately help reduce Treasury's overall cost of funding by attracting a new pool of investors and facilitate better liability management."

There is direct evidence that TIPS could help Treasury access different groups of investors.[15] According to research by a New York Federal Reserve expert on Treasury markets, between July 30, 2001, and December 28, 2005, investment funds (which included mutual funds and hedge funds) accounted for 30.2 percent of TIPS sold at auction, but only 11.5 percent of nominal notes and bonds.[16] Whereas, between July 30, 2001, and December 28, 2005, the largest group of Treasury holders, foreign and international investors, accounted for 8.2 percent of TIPS sold at auction and 21.1 percent of nominal notes and bonds. Another example of the diversification that TIPS could provide is that pension funds tend to purchase a higher share of TIPS securities than nominal Treasury securities at auctions.

While TIPS auctions have been highly concentrated, with just a few regular participants, TIPS may exhibit less ownership concentration than nominal securities. As of December 2008, the largest TIPS fund (Vanguard Inflation-Protected Securities Fund) reported $16.6 billion in TIPS holdings, accounting for 3.1 percent of the $530 billion in TIPS outstanding on that date. In contrast, Treasury International Capital data shows that the largest foreign holder of U.S. Treasury securities (China) reported $727 billion, accounting for 12.5 percent of the $5.8 trillion in total marketable Treasury securities on the same date.[17]

One indicator of TIPS' potential to diversify funding sources for Treasury is the growth of inflation-protected mutual funds. Both the number and the amount of assets under management in inflation-protected funds have increased since 2002. As seen in figure 8, the number of inflation-protected funds doubled from 20 at the end of December 2002 to 40 at the end of May 2009. The amounts of inflation-protected funds under management increased from $11.8 billion to $54.4 billion during the same period. The mutual fund managers that we interviewed expressed their investors' continued interest in the TIPS program going forward and plan to continue to purchase TIPS securities over the next year. According to data from one large mutual fund company, between 2003 and 2008 the large majority of inflows into its TIPS fund came from non-Treasury funds.

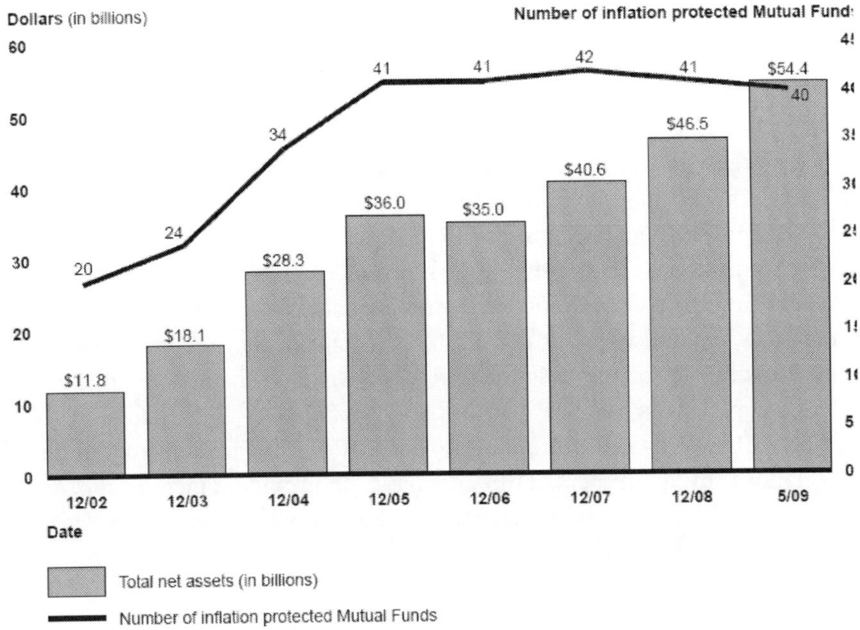


Source: GAO analysis of Investment Company Institute data.

Figure 8. Inflation-Protected Mutual Funds and Assets under Management, December 2002 to May 2009.

According to market experts, another potential benefit of the TIPS program to Treasury is its potential to reduce government borrowing costs. If Treasury has to increase the supply of nominal securities substantially to fund larger deficits, it may need to raise yields in order to attract enough buyers due to the saturation of the nominal Treasury market. Therefore, issuing TIPS may make sense as a substantial shift in the composition of Treasury issuance into TIPS from nominal Treasuries could lead to lower interest rates paid on the remaining nominal Treasury issuance. This argument has been cited as a benefit by a number of market experts, but additional research is required. Treasury's access to auction data puts ODM staff in a unique position to conduct a comprehensive and ongoing analysis of the impact that TIPS have on the cost of nominal securities. In commenting on this report, Treasury told us that ODM staff have reviewed such data. They note that TIPS have remained less liquid than nominal securities and are considering approaches to improve the inflation-indexed market.

Treasury securities have the potential to provide a number of social, fiscal, and monetary benefits. All Treasury securities provide investors with virtually zero credit risk. Only TIPS, however, provide zero inflation risk, making them one of the most effective ways for risk-averse households to meet their savings needs. In contrast, one of the downsides of nominal Treasury securities is that in the event of unexpected inflation, the real return to investors will be less than expected. Investors in nominal Treasury securities assume the risk of inflation eroding their expected return, but inflation-protected investments, such as TIPS, shift the inflation risk to the issuer.

Economists have noted that governments are better able to bear inflation risk because periods of inflation are often associated with increased revenues. Economists have also noted that TIPS could make the Federal government more accountable for the inflationary consequences of its actions in the form of higher payments on TIPS, if inflation increases. The results of TIPS auctions also provide useful information to policymakers on inflation expectations. In this respect, TIPS auctions help provide a measure of market inflation expectations, which can be taken into account when making monetary policy decisions.[18]

## Forward-Looking Analysis of TIPS Program's Costs Adds an Important Perspective to Evaluating the Role of TIPS as Part of Treasury's Debt Portfolio

Market experts have measured costs of TIPS in two primary ways. The first approach evaluates TIPS on an ex-post (after the fact) basis. That is, the cost of TIPS and nominal securities are compared based on what inflation actually was during a given time period.[19] Economists conducting ex-post analyses have concluded that the TIPS program has been less cost-effective for Treasury than nominal securities. A 2008 study by a Federal Reserve economist estimated that the total cost of the TIPS program through October 2007 was between \$4.5 billion and \$7.5 billion.[20] Based on TIPS issued through July 2009, Treasury's ODM estimated the total cost of TIPS at \$10 billion to date. This more recent study includes the anomalous period characterized by the financial market crisis and the related flight to quality which made nominal securities relatively inexpensive for Treasury. Economists generally agree that part of the relatively higher cost of the TIPS program can be attributed to its start-up costs. According to market experts and the major institutional investors that we interviewed, other factors that may have contributed to the relatively higher cost to Treasury of the TIPS program to date are investors' perceptions of Treasury's lack of commitment to the program and the relatively low inflation experienced throughout the life of the program. Since the TIPS program was introduced, the annual Consumer Price Index for All Urban Consumers (CPI-U) percent change never exceeded 3.8 percent, which is low by historical standards. The CPI-U averaged 7.08 percent and 5.55 percent during the 1970s and 1980s, respectively.

**Ex-ante vs. Ex-post Analysis**

**Ex-ante** is Latin for beforehand. In models with uncertainty, ex-ante values are expected values that are calculated before the uncertainty is resolved.

**Ex-**post is Latin for after the fact. In models with uncertainty, ex-post values are the realized or actual values that are calculated after the uncertainty has been resolved.

In the context of nominal interest-bearing government securities, investors are assumed to demand compensation for expected inflation. Ex-ante expectations about inflation are assumed to be formed rationally, meaning that expectations will be identical to optimal forecasts using all available information. Ex-post, realized inflation rates may differ from ex-ante expected values, but these differences should not be systematically positive or negative.

For a sufficiently lengthy time horizon the cost of TIPS relative to nominal Treasury securities should be the same when calculated on both an ex-ante and ex-post basis, all else equal. For shorter time horizons, the difference between expected and realized inflation values may appear to be persistent; thus, the ex-ante approach may be preferred to assess the cost of TIPS relative to nominal Treasury securities over the short term.

In contrast, other economists who have studied the issue argue that from an ex-ante (before the fact) basis, TIPS are not more costly to issue than nominal securities and that the relative cost of the TIPS program to date in part reflects start-up costs that will not be incurred again.[21] One recent study by

Treasury's ODM found that TIPS are not less costly when measured on an ex-ante basis, but this study includes the anomalous period characterized by the financial market crisis and the related flight to quality which made nominal securities relatively inexpensive for Treasury. Another ex-ante study, noted that if the TIPS program were as liquid as the market for off-the-run nominal Treasuries, Treasury would have realized total cost savings from the TIPS program of $22 billion to $32 billion.[22] Over the short run, economists recognize that an assessment of TIPS program's relative costs depends on whether Treasury or the investor is the beneficiary from differences in expected and actual inflation. The time horizon of the analysis affects the results since, over the long run, the average amount by which actual inflation exceeds expected inflation will roughly equal the average amount when the opposite is true.[23] Therefore, some market experts argue that TIPS should be evaluated on an ex-ante basis, for example, by finding the difference between the breakeven inflation rate (the nominal-TIPS yield differential) and a survey-based measure of inflation expectations at the time of the TIPS auction. This difference is independent of inflation surprises and provides a measure of the net savings or loss incurred by Treasury.

## CONCLUDING OBSERVATIONS

Faced with the economic recession and the ensuing 2008 financial market crisis, Treasury is to be commended for its success in raising unprecedented amounts of cash in a very short amount of time. Absent policy changes, the medium- and long-term fiscal outlook mean that Treasury will need to raise increasing amounts of cash, and build borrowing flexibility by increasing the term to maturity of its debt portfolio, while retaining its focus on reducing its overall borrowing cost. While questions remain about how to evaluate the cost of the TIPS program, TIPS have the potential to provide Treasury with a number of benefits and help Treasury achieve its debt management objectives.

On July 1, 2009, we briefed Treasury's ODM on the findings from our analysis and interviews with major institutional investors. Treasury later posed questions about ways to improve the TIPS program to the Primary Dealers and TBAC. At the August 2009 TBAC meeting, members discussed TIPS. Following the meeting, Treasury's Deputy Assistant Secretary for Federal Finance reaffirmed Treasury's commitment to TIPS and announced plans to gradually increase issuance of TIPS.

## RECOMMENDATIONS

The Secretary of the Treasury should take the following actions to improve TIPS liquidity in the context of projected sustained increases in federal debt:

- increase TIPS issuance,
- issue TIPS with longer-dated maturities, and
- conduct more frequent TIPS auctions.

The Secretary should continually review the appropriate composition of the TIPS program, and consider:

- the impact of Treasury's public statements and TIPS issuances on TIPS liquidity,
- how both ex-ante (before the fact) and ex-post (after the fact) analyses are valuable for evaluating the cost of TIPS, recognizing the anomalous nature of market data from periods such as the 2008 financial market crisis,
- the ways in which the TIPS program can diversify Treasury's investor base and funding sources, and
- the degree to which TIPS impact the cost of nominal securities.

## AGENCY COMMENTS

We requested comments on a draft of this report from the Secretary of the Treasury and received comments on behalf of the Treasury from its Deputy Assistant Secretary of Federal Finance. Treasury took note of our findings, conclusions, and recommendations, and said they were consistent with their commitment to increasing TIPS issuance in the context of projected sustained increases in federal debt. Treasury reiterated that they are committed to issuing TIPS in a regular and predictable manner across the yield curve, and noted that they are an important part of their overall debt management strategy. Treasury also noted that it is always reviewing the appropriate composition of the TIPS program.

Sincerely yours,

Susan J. Irving
Director, Federal Budget Analysis
Strategic Issues

# APPENDIX I: TREASURY INFLATION PROTECTED SECURITIES

## Overview

Treasury Inflation Protected Securities (TIPS) are marketable securities for which the principal is adjusted by changes in the Consumer Price Index for All Urban Consumers (CPI-U).[1] With inflation (a rise in the index), the principal increases. With deflation (a drop in the index), the principal decreases for the purpose of calculating interest payments, but the principal to be repaid at maturity is at least par value (or the principal amount at date of original issuance). Although the inflation-adjusted principal is paid by the Department of the Treasury when the security matures, interest payments are made every 6 months. TIPS are the only Treasury security that secures the investor a return on the investment that is guaranteed in purchasing power terms rather than in dollar terms.

## Principal

At maturity, Treasury pays investors the greater of the inflation-adjusted principal amount or the par value. That is, investors are protected against both increases in inflation and the loss of the original principal. During the lifetime of a TIPS, the principal could decline with deflation below the original par value, so the coupon payment could fall below their originally stated dollar amounts, but at maturity the principal will be redeemed at no less than the original face amount.

---

[1] The index for the inflation rate is the Bureau of Labor Statistic's nonseasonally adjusted U.S. City Average All Items Consumer Price Index for All Urban Consumers (CPI-U). TIPS are indexed to a lagged value of the CPI by 3 months, rather than the contemporaneous value.

## Interest Payments

Interest is paid every 6 months at a fixed rate, which was determined at auction when the security was first sold. However, because the rate is applied to the adjusted principal, interest payments may vary from one period to another. Interest payments are based on the inflation-adjusted principal on the date of the interest payment.[2] In a period of inflation, the principal is adjusted upward so the interest payment increases. In the event of deflation, the principal is adjusted downward, and the interest payment decreases.[3]

Below is an illustrative example of how to calculate the inflation adjustments to the principal and the semi-annual interest payments (note that CPI-U numbers and rates are purely hypothetical).

## Taxation

Both interest payments and the inflation adjustments applied to the principal of TIPS are subject to federal tax. The accrued increase in principal caused by the inflation adjustment is taxable in the year in which it is accrued, which is the standard structure for all other Treasury securities. However, with TIPS the increase in principal is an unrealized gain because the principal is not received until the bond matures. This is not an issue if TIPS are held in a tax-deferred account.

## Auction Schedule

Treasury currently auctions 5-, 10-, and 20-year TIPS. Treasury used to also issue 30-year TIPS, but discontinued doing so in 2001. Treasury currently auctions TIPS on a quarterly basis. The 5-year TIPS is issued in April and reopened in October.[4] The 10-year TIPS is issued in January and July, with

[2] The amount of each interest payment is determined by multiplying the adjusted principal by one-half the interest rate.

[3] Even though the principal is adjusted downward for the purpose of the calculation of interest payments, the original principal amount on the date of issuance is returned to the investor at maturity.

[4] In a reopening, Treasury sells an additional amount of a previously issued security. The reopened security has the same maturity date and interest rate as the original security.

reopenings in April and October, and the 20-year TIPS is issued in January and reopened in July.

**How to Calculate an Inflation-Indexed Security Interest and Principal**

An inflation-indexed security with par value of $1,000,000 was purchased on April 15, 2003, with a coupon rate of 3.5 percent. The first semi-annual interest payment date for this inflation indexed security is October 15, 2003. The reference CPI-U number for the issue date was 120. The reference CPI-U number for the first interest payment was 135.

The inflation adjusted principal on October 15, 2003 was:

$1,000,000 x 135/120 = $1,125,000

The interest payment was:

$1,125,000 x 0.035/2 = $19,687.50

## Purchasing TIPS

TIPS are sold in increments of $100, with a required minimum purchase of $100. Treasury issues TIPS in electronic form. At auction, an investor can place competitive or noncompetitive bids for TIPS. However, noncompetitive bids are limited in a single auction to $5 million while competitive bids are limited to 35 percent of the initial offering amount.[5] Investors can hold TIPS until they mature or sell them in the secondary market before they mature.

However, as compared to the original security, the reopened security has a different issue date and can have a different purchase price.

5 [5]A competitive bid is a bid to U.S. Treasury to buy Treasury securities at a particular yield. A noncompetitive bid is a method of purchasing Treasury securities at auction, without having to submit a price or a yield. Unlike competitive bids, noncompetitive bids are always accepted. [2]Ingo Fender, Corrinne Ho, and Peter Hordähl, "Overview: investors ponder depth and duration of global downturn," *BIS Quarterly Review* (March 2009).

# APPENDIX II: THE COST OF TREASURY INFLATION PROTECTED SECURITIES COMPARED TO NOMINAL SECURITIES

For a sufficiently lengthy time horizon the cost of Treasury Inflation Protected Securities (TIPS) relative to nominal Treasury securities should be the same when calculated on both an ex-ante (before the fact) and ex-post (after the fact) basis, all else equal.

The following arithmetic illustrates the approximate equivalence between ex-ante and ex-post evaluations of the cost of TIPS relative to nominal securities.[6]

**Ex-Post Calculation of the Nominal-TIPS Cost Difference**

Nominal yield = real yield + expected inflation + inflation risk premium

TIPS yield = real yield + illiquidity premium

Ex-post evaluation of the cost difference between nominals and TIPS adds actual inflation to the TIPS yield, so ex-post:

TIPS yield = real yield + illiquidity premium + actual inflation
Ex-post, therefore, the nominal-TIPS cost difference is:

real yield + expected inflation + inflation risk premium –
real yield - illiquidity premium - actual inflation
In the long run, expected inflation should equal actual inflation on average, so the ex-post nominal-TIPS cost difference reduces to:

inflation risk premium - illiquidity premium

Ex-ante calculation of the cost difference between nominals and TIPS subtracts a survey-based measure of expected inflation from the nominal-TIPS cost difference.

---

6 While the cost difference between nominal Treasury securities and TIPS is primarily driven by illiquidity and inflation risk premiums, the relative cost also reflects such technical market factors as the taxation difference between TIPS and nominal issuances, the convexity of difference between real and nominal yields, and the price of TIPS embedded deflation floor.

> Ex-Ante Calculation of the Nominal-TIPS Cost Difference
>
> Real yield + expected inflation + inflation risk premium – surveyed inflation
> expectation - real yield - illiquidity premium
>
> If the survey accurately captures expected inflation, then expected inflation equals surveyed expected inflation and this ex-ante difference reduces to:
>
> Inflation risk premium - illiquidity premium

Again, over the long run, if expected inflation = surveyed expected inflation = actual inflation, ex-ante and ex-post calculations of the cost of TIPS relative to nominals should be approximately the same. However, the possibility of persistent inflation surprises in one direction over a few years suggests using the ex-ante approach over shorter horizons.

## DISENTANGLING THE DRIVERS OF RECENT SHIFTS IN THE NOMINAL-TIPS YIELD DIFFERENTIAL (BREAKEVEN INFLATION RATE)

The cost of TIPS compared to nominal securities increased substantially in fall 2008 when the subprime crisis intensified.[2] During the latter part of 2008, TIPS yields rose while nominal yields declined resulting in near historic lows in the breakeven inflation rate, approaching zero by the end of 2008. During 2009, breakeven rates generally rose from their late-2008 lows and reached the 2 percent range in early August.

> **Disentangling the Drivers of Recent Shifts in the Nominal-TIPS Yield Differential (Breakeven Inflation Rate)**
>
> The sharp decline in breakeven inflation rates in late 2008 can be attributed to a combination of liquidity and technical market factors. Strong flight-to-liquidity flows during the market upheaval boosted the demand for nominal Treasury securities. Because TIPS markets are less liquid than nominal Treasury markets, this reduced the breakeven inflation rate.

In addition, technical market factors closely linked to liquidity effects appear to have contributed to the decline in breakeven inflation rates. Lehman Brothers owned TIPS as part of repo trades or posted TIPS as counterparty collateral. Because of Lehman's bankruptcy, the court and its counterparty needed to sell these TIPS, which created a flood of TIPS on the market. There appeared to be few buyers and distressed market makers were unwilling to take positions in these TIPS. As a result, the TIPS yields rose sharply.

Inflation expectations and the inflation risk premium, two other important determinants of the nominal-TIPS yield differential, appear to have had negligible roles in the recent shifts in the yield differential. The median survey value of 10-year inflation forecasts compiled by the Federal Reserve Bank of Philadelphia's Survey of Professional Forecasters displayed little variation over the last 2 years, which implies that long-term inflation expectations remained stable. Estimates also suggest that the inflation risk premium has remained relatively small and fairly stable.

Some financial economists view the experience with TIPS yields after the Lehman bankruptcy as a highly abnormal market situation where liquidity issues suddenly created severe financial anomalies. They suggest that this was an unrepresentative episode and that observations from this period could be ignored.

See John Campbell, Robert Shiller, and Luis Viceira, "Understanding Inflation-Indexed Bond Markets," *Working Paper Presented Brookings Institute* (March 2009); and Ingo Fender, Corrinne Ho, and Peter Hordähl, "Overview: investors ponder depth and duration of global downturn," *BIS Quarterly Review* (March 2009).

## End Notes

[1] As of the end of 2008, inflation-indexed securities made up 24 percent of the United Kingdom's total outstanding debt portfolio, 15 percent of France's outstanding debt portfolio, and 10 percent of the United States' outstanding debt portfolio.

[2] ODM is responsible for providing the Assistant Secretary for Financial Markets with advice and analysis on matters related to the Treasury's debt management policy, the issuance of Treasury and federally related securities, and financial markets.

[3] Federal debt held by the public is the value of all federal securities sold to the public that are still outstanding. See GAO, *Federal Debt: Answers to Frequently Asked Questions: An Update*, GAO-04-485SP (Washington, D.C.: August 12, 2004).

[4] Treasury issues two major types of debt securities to the public: marketable and nonmarketable securities. Marketable securities, which consist of Treasury bills, notes, and bonds and can

be resold by whoever owns them while nonmarketable securities, such as savings securities and special securities for state and local governments, cannot be resold.

[5] Treasury data states that almost half of the $6.6 trillion in marketable securities is held by foreign investors, as of May 2009.

[6] Treasury's increase in issuance of cash management bills is largely due to establishment of the Supplementary Financing Program (SFP). The SFP was created to provide cash for Federal Reserve lending and liquidity draining initiatives in response to the financial market crisis. According to GAO's audit of the Bureau of the Public Debt for Fiscal Years 2008 and 2007, $300 billion in cash management bills were issued in September 2008 under the Supplementary Financing Program initiated by Treasury. See GAO, *Financial Audit: Bureau of the Public Debt's Fiscal Years 2008 and 2007 Schedules of Federal Debt*, GAO-09-44 (Washington, D.C.: November 7, 2008).

[7] See Congressional Budget Office, *An Analysis of the President's Budgetary Proposals for Fiscal Year 2010* (Washington, D.C.: June 2009).

[8] As of August 2009, the average maturity of issuance on the current auction calendar now exceeds the average maturity of marketable debt outstanding.

[9] See GAO, *The Nation's Long-Term Fiscal Outlook March 2009 Update,* GAO-09-405SP (Washington, D.C.: April 30, 2009) and CBO, *The Long-Term Budget Outlook* (Washington, D.C.: June 2009).

[10] At the August 2009 Treasury Borrowing Advisory Committee (TBAC) meeting, Treasury asked TBAC members to consider whether 30-year TIPS should replace 20-year TIPS. 30-year TIPS would also serve to reduce the amount of securities that Treasury needs to roll over in the next 10 years.

[11] We use the real-time estimate of expected inflation from the Survey of Professional Forecasters maintained by the Federal Reserve Bank of Philadelphia.

[12] The bid-to-cover ratio is the ratio between the amounts tendered over the amounts accepted at auction.

[13] Gross issuance is the total amount issued in a year (whether it is obtaining new money or refinancing maturing debt). As we have shown, it has decreased since 2006. The net change in total TIPS outstanding from year to year increased during this time, but at a decreasing rate (reflecting the decrease in gross issuance). In commenting on this report, Treasury's Director of ODM and ODM staff said that they view this as a stabilization of the TIPS program—done to permit a review of the program after its first decade.

[14] SIFMA is an organization that represents the shared interests of participants in the global financial markets. SIFMA members include international securities firms, U.S.-registered broker-dealers and asset managers. SIFMA members are part of TBAC, which meets quarterly with Treasury and presents their observations to Treasury on the overall strength of the U.S. economy as well as providing recommendations on a variety of technical debt management issues.

[15] As investors can purchase TIPS in either the secondary market or at auction, diversification of Treasury's end-user investor base might not be directly related to auction concentration.

[16] Michael Fleming, "Who Buys Treasury Securities at Auction?" *Current Issues in Economics and Finance*, vol. 13, no. 1 (2007).

[17] Treasury International Capital data is available at http://www.treasury.gov/tic.

[18] William C. Dudley, Jennifer Roush, and Michelle Steinberg Ezer, "The Case for TIPS: An Examination of the Costs and Benefits," *FRBNY Economic Policy Review* (July 2009).

[19] For the total cost of the TIPS program, ex-post analysis computes the cost of TIPS going forward if future inflation follows an assumed path.

[20] Jennifer Roush, "The 'Growing Pains' of TIPS Issuance," *Finance and Economic Discussion Series* (2008).

[21] Jennifer Roush, "The 'Growing Pains' of TIPS Issuance," *Finance and Economic Discussion Series* (2008); William C. Dudley, Jennifer Roush, and Michelle Steinberg Ezer, "The Case for TIPS: An Examination of the Costs and Benefits," *FRBNY Economic Policy Review* (July 2009); and Pu Shen, "Developing a Liquid Market for Inflation-Indexed Government Securities: Lessons from Earlier Experiences," *Economic Review* (First Quarter 2009).

[22] Off-the-run securities are securities that are no longer on-the-run (or the most recently auctioned security of a given maturity).

[23] William C. Dudley, Jennifer Roush, and Michelle Steinberg Ezer, "The Case for TIPS: An Examination of the Costs and Benefits," *FRBNY Economic Policy Review* (July 2009); and Dean Croushore, "An Evaluation of Inflation Forecasts From Surveys Using Real-Time Data," *Federal Reserve Bank of Philadelphia Working Papers* (December 2008).

# INDEX

## D

## G



## H



## I



## J



## L

## V



## W



## Y